旅游语篇语用顺应翻译研究

闫凤霞 著

中国海洋大学出版社
·青岛·

图书在版编目（CIP）数据

旅游语篇语用顺应翻译研究：英语／闫凤霞著．--
青岛：中国海洋大学出版社，2021. 11
ISBN 978-7-5670-2948-4

Ⅰ．①旅… Ⅱ．①闫… Ⅲ．①旅游－英语－翻译－研
究 Ⅳ．① F59

中国版本图书馆 CIP 数据核字（2021）第 206484 号

出版发行	中国海洋大学出版社
社　　址	青岛市香港东路 23 号　　　　邮政编码　266071
出 版 人	杨立敏
网　　址	http://pub.ouc.edu.cn
电子信箱	1922305382@qq.com
订购电话	0532-82032573（传真）
责任编辑	邵成军　　　　　　　　　电　　话　0532-85902533
印　　制	日照日报印务中心
版　　次	2021 年 11 月第 1 版
印　　次	2021 年 11 月第 1 次印刷
成品尺寸	170 mm ×230 mm
印　　张	9.75
字　　数	220 千
印　　数	1～1 000
定　　价	45.00 元

CONTENTS

Chapter 1
Introduction

1.1 Research Background

1.1.1 Current Situation of Tourism in the World

Nowadays tourism has become the fastest booming tertiary industry in the world. It could stimulate domestic demands, provide job opportunities and increase financial revenues. It is predicted by the World Travel and Tourism Council that tourism in the 21st century will become the world's largest booming industry with no tendency of deceleration. From 2010 to 2020, the number of international tourism and international tourism revenue had grown at an average annual rate of 4.3% and 6.7% respectively, higher than the 3% average annual growth rate of world wealth in the same period. By 2020, tourism revenues had grown to $16 trillion, equivalent to 10% of global Gross Domestic Product (GDP). It has provided 300 million jobs, accounting for 9.2% of the world's total employment, further strengthening its position in the global economy. Based on a report issued by the China Tourism Academy, 4.1 billion domestic tourist trips will be carried out in China in 2021 with an increase of 42% from 2020. In addition, domestic tourism revenue is estimated to surge 48% to reach 3.3 trillion yuan (about $503 billion). What lies behind these figures is the potential huge tourism market. Tourism not only basically means relaxation from the busy life as people always think, but also is an important job provider with nearly 100 million vacancies. Research indicates that job creation in tourism is growing 1.5 times faster than any other industrial sector. Furthermore, most jobs are provided in underdeveloped countries where tourism turns out a major source of income in those countries, which will push forward the tourist destination's economy. Tourism is also an important means to attract investment. Investment at home and abroad on the infrastructure and other facilities like airport, road, and real estate will promote the living standard and life quality of the local people. In addition, the tourism industry supplies government with millions of dollars in tax revenues through accommodation and restaurant taxes, airport fees, sales taxes, park entrance fees, employee income tax and many other fiscal revenues. International and domestic tourism industry combined generate up to 10% of the world's GDP and a considerably higher share in many small nations and developing countries. Even in many countries, it ranks among the top three industries; as for employment, it is second to health services. Take the United States as an example. According to the U.S. Travel Data Center, during the past 10 years, tourism employment in the United States has grown by 56.3% and now totals over 6 million direct jobs. This is more than twice the job rate increase for the American economy as a whole.

The burgeoning tourism can be associated with a variety of factors. The recovered economy after the World War II ensured people of paid leave from employment and disposable income. Convenient transportation, especially the use of jet aircraft since the 1960s, facilitates the communication between countries. Meanwhile, the lowered price of plane tickets lures people to travel around. The comparatively stable political environment makes increasing people feel safe abroad. Europe becomes the dominant host region, followed by North America, Asia, the Pacific, Africa, and the Middle East. Ever since the 21st century, the fabric of tourism changes tremendously. Asia rises to the second place, making up a tourism triangle with Europe and America. As a tourism giant in Asia, China's tourism development is noteworthy. Modern Chinese tourism is booming so fast that many scholars call it "China Phenomenon."

1.1.2 Modern Tourism in China

China is a magnificent country with a history of over 5,000 years. Its ancient temples, delicate silk and china, and beautiful landscapes capture the attention of tourists. The snow-covered mountains, vast-spread grassland and nomadic horse-riders pose great challenges to foreign adventurers. Since ancient times, China has remained a mystery for many foreigners to explore the traditional Chinese culture.

Modern tourism in China experiences three periods. At the beginning, the first travel agency was established in November, 1949. After five years, the China International Travel Service was founded with 14 branches in Guangzhou, Shanghai, Beijing and other major cities. In 1964, the National Tourism Administration of China was officially established, which pushed the national tourism into prosperity. However, during the so-called Cultural Revolution, tourism halted for the known political reasons until the revolution was over. In these periods, tourism was carried out unofficially. It played an important role in publicizing the achievement of the People's Republic of China and strengthening the communications between nations. However, due to lack of fund and facilities, tourism at that time was developed in a small scale with a simplified structure.

Then, after 1978, under the direction of Deng Xiaoping, who put forward a series of visions on tourism economy including environment preservation, construction of tourism facilities, tourism management, improvement of tourism service and tourist goods, modern Chinese tourism took on a new look and roared to one of the fastest growing industry. The National Tourism Bureaucracy reported that in 2005, the number of inbound tourists reached 1.2 billion with 4.68 million more than one-night tourists, showing an increase of 10% and 12% respectively. The annual tourism revenue increased by 13% with a total income of $269 billion.

After that, since China's entry into World Trade Organization (WTO), the speedy economy makes prerequisites for the tourism development; relatively stable political environment ensures tourists' safety in traveling, especially after the "9.11 Incident," most tourists prefer a safe and peaceful destination. When the successful cultural tour between China and France ended, another rounds of cultural tour between China and Russia, China and India got started in series. Those official cultural tours shorten the distance between nations and will definitely promote the friendship between China and European or other Asian countries. In addition, when the 2008 Olympic Games was held in Beijing, a growing number of people went to China to watch this magnificent game. Anything related to this game, such as the tourist byproducts, slogans, advertisement, has propelled the development of tourism.

Lacking of facilities, ineffective infrastructure, and inflexible business operation prevent tourism from coming into full play. Services in tourism are not so qualified that they damage the image of the destinations. In tourism text translation—one of tourist products, mistakes of various kinds are often found to hamper the ongoing cross-cultural communication. To solve this problem, the author will center on tourism text translation and try to analyze the causes of translation errors and then provide translation strategies in order to shed light on the translation theory and practice.

1.2 Objectives of the Research

The booming tourism industry calls for the high-quality tourism translation products to publicize the traditional Chinese culture and attract more foreign tourists to pay a visit. However, lacking of unified guided translation theory and corresponding laws and regulations, linguistic, cultural and pragmatic mistakes pop up in tourism text translation damaging the image of the travel destination. In order to provide a theoretical panoramic view on tourism text translation, the author proposes a model on tourism text translation under the framework of Verschueren's Adaptation Theory. In addition, a survey on translation of scenic spots located mainly in Shandong Province was conducted to answer the following questions:

(1) How does adaptation to the structures function in tourism text translation?

(2) How does adaptation to the physical world function in tourism text translation?

(3) How does adaptation to the mental world function in tourism text

translation?

(4) How does adaptation to the social world function in tourism text translation?

(5) What are the translation strategies in tourism text?

1.3   Data Collection and Methodology

The corpora that the author uses in this thesis derive from the following sources: the pictorials, handbooks, pamphlets and public notices and signs issued by the government, tourist bureau, travel agency and internet sites. Each quotation from the sources is marked by the author. For the convenience of investigation, the author divides all the corpora into four categories, i.e., adaptation to structural, physical, social and mental worlds respectively. Furthermore, a survey on scenic spots translation is attached in the thesis to investigate how those correlates are taking effects in tourism text translation. On the basis of the survey, the translation strategies are provided to guarantee the acceptability of the versions. The research method in the thesis is mainly a combination of qualitative and quantitative methods.

1.4   Structure of the Thesis

The thesis comprises nine chapters.

Chapter 1 is an introduction.

Chapter 2 is a literature review of relevant studies on tourism text translation. Firstly, definition, classification and functions of tourism texts are clarified to confine the scope of the research. Secondly, the author reviews the development of tourism text translation at home and abroad. Thirdly, a review of Adaptation Theory is offered. Meanwhile, the author summarizes the present problems in tourism text translation.

Chapter 3 is the theoretical framework. Key concepts in Adaptation Theory, such as making choices, three key notions and four angles of investigation are clarified to show how they impact the translation process. Then the author proposes her translation model under the framework of Adaptation Theory and points out the theoretical and practical significance. After that, the author points out the methodology of the thesis and the results based on the survey the author conducted in tourism text translation versions.

Chapters 4 to 7 account for the adaptability in tourism text translation. The author specifies tourism text translation in respect of structural, physical, mental and social worlds by using bilingual translation versions. She finds that adaptability plays an important role in translating the above correlates.

In Chapter 8, the author proposes specific translation strategies including transliteration, adding, omission, analogy and other translation methods. Those strategies demonstrate the translators' passive and active adaptation to the foreign tourists' linguistic, physical, social and mental settings. In these ways, foreign tourists' needs in travelling can be best fulfilled.

The last chapter is the conclusion part of the thesis. The author summarizes the implications of the thesis and defines the future research scope. At the same time, she points out the limitations of the present research.

Chapter 2
Literature Review

2.1 Definition, Classification and Functions of Tourism Text

2.1.1 Definition

Before giving the definition of tourism text, we should firstly make clear what tourism is. However, defining tourism is no easy job. There is no universally acknowledged concept of tourism because what constitutes tourism is still a matter of debate. The term "tourism" first appeared in the *Oxford Dictionary* in 1811, which meant paying a visit to one or more places before going home. It was a superficial description of tourism. After that, more tourism institutions and organizations made efforts to further the study on tourism. There are different views concerning the definition of tourism. One of the influential views held by the WTO in 1991 claimed that tourism comprised the activities of persons traveling to and staying in places outside their usual environment for not more than one consecutive year. It aimed for leisure, business and other purposes, not related to the exercise of an organized activity remunerated within the place visited. Here "outside their usual environment" excluded tours between the living place and the work site, tours inside the living place and regular tours. "Not more than one consecutive year" implied that tour occurred in a short period. Therefore, tourism was a temporary activity to another place whose aim is not for job attainment. In this thesis, the author defines tourism as a trans-cultural and trans-psychological process which encompasses food, accommodation, transportation, traveling, shopping and entertainment activities.

With millions of dollars generated in income, tourism is regarded as an industry. It is a collection of business activities including food, accommodation, transport, shopping and entertainment. It also contains tour wholesalers, retailers and a variety of tourist attractions, as well as other private and public services and facilities. Gilbert (1990) argued that tourism required a range of non-industrial resources which laid foundations for the tourism products. Such non-industrial resources include climate, scenery, beaches, wildlife and the culture of the host community. As time goes by, the nature and functions of tourism arouse more and more scholars' interest. Tourism has been established as a new branch of discipline and become specialized. Things related to tourism, such as tourism products, travelers, marketing and psychology in tourism, tourism economy, tourism text, become the research object of the tourist scholars. In this thesis, the author only focuses on a special genre of tourism—tourism text.

Tourism texts are materials intended to introduce the destination's resources, products, entertainment, transport, travel agencies, hotels, etc. They can be in both written and oral forms. Oral texts refer to those materials used in interpreting, such as on-the-way interpretation, on-the-spot interpretation, but these texts are not what we concern about in this thesis. Written texts are mainly tourism publicity materials. Tourism publicity materials are issued through a certain channel, standard or non-standard, either by tourist bureau, by the travel agency itself or by internet. They provide information on the tourist attraction and exhibit the unique culture so as to attract more tourists to visit the country. Tourism texts deepen tourists' understanding on the culture of the destination, arouse tourists' interests and motivate them to go outside. Nowadays tourism texts play an increasingly important role in the cross-cultural communication.

2.1.2 Classification

Tourism texts cover a wide range of substances including tourism brochures, pamphlets, tourist guide, advertising, tourist slogans and signs, tourist maps, notices and announcements, hotel menus, names of scenic spots and so on. Besides, tourist pictorials, and postcards are also included in this category. Sometimes, pictures and paintings are attached to introduce the destination vividly. For the convenience of further research, the author divides the tourism materials as follows.

2.1.2.1   Tourist Guide

Tourist guide is a special tourism genre which provides tourists with detailed information on the scenic spots: hotel, routes, expenses, recreational activities, travel arrangement, etc. The major function of tourist guide is informative, but sometimes it is colored with description and persuasiveness. Zhang Delu (1998) subdivided tourist guide into three categories: tourist service guide, scenic spot description and travel introduction.

Travel service guide offers travel services and conditions to the would-be tourists. Therefore, much detailed information is needed, such as the hotel condition, route, expenses and the ways to contact with the guide and host. It is characterized by the list of particular figures, facts and necessities in traveling. The language is plain with short and elliptical sentences.

Scenic spot description gives vivid information on a particular scenic place. It includes the information about the facilities, travel services and the description of the particular scenic spot. As a result, it is informative as well as vivid and persuasive. Perceptive, evaluative and exaggerating words and expressions are employed in the description.

Travel introduction will provide tourists with the general information about how to travel. Special language patterns are introduced to achieve the functions of directions, advice and suggestions. So imperative clauses and declarative clauses with the directive effect, and clauses with modal verbs feature this kind of writing. Here is an illustration of tourist guide:

Example 2-1   Blessed with excellent transportation facilities, it takes only ten minutes by car to get to the renowned scenic spot named Splendid China from Luomazhou Post. The spot is easy of access both by CTS direct tourist coach between Hong Kong and Shenzhen and by bus or light bus through Shen-Nan Highway, Guang-Shen Highway and Beihuan Freeway.

Welcome to Splendid China.

(Extracted from Baidu Wenku)

2.1.2.2　Advertisement

Today advertisement is widespread in people's life through TV, radio or magazines. It permeates nearly every working field, such as cosmetics, cars, medicine, food and drinks. Tourism is no exception. In *Random House Webster's Dictionary of American English* (1997), advertisement is "a paid notice or announcement, as of goods for sale, in newspapers or magazines, on radio or television, etc." The purpose of making advertisement is to sell goods, thus the language of advertisement could be very vivid in order to attract the readers' attention and finally persuade them to buy the product. Advertisement varies in content and form. Some are printed in newspapers or magazines, and others come from television, radio or internet. The format of advertisements could be simple or complex, sometimes with drawings and pictures to draw people's attention. The main function of advertisement is informative, entertaining and most of all, persuasive to the consumers in order to reach a deal. In tourism text, good advertisement will share the following features.

Be informative. Advertisement is a special means to make the tourists aware of all the information about the destinations. No matter how charming and florid an advertisement is, what the future tourists concern about are the necessities of the tour, including the accommodation, itinerary, fees and ways of transportation. Therefore, for successful tourism advertisers, the primary and most important thing to bear in mind is trying to be informative.

Be appealing. Nowadays, advertisement is seen everywhere on TV, radio and in magazines. It occurs so often and unexpectedly that many people hate it at the first sight. By contrast, a carefully designed advertisement is a different matter. It will arouse consumers' attention on the spot. Thus, an advertiser should come up with the latest tide and specify where the consumers' interest lies.

Be persuasive. The use of advertisements intends to lead the readers to the final buying action. Some superlative adjectives, modal words such as "should, must, better" are in use to ensure tourists of the high qualities of the future products. Next is an advertisement of Greece.

Example 2-2   A perfect stay of comfort, beauty and nature,

Want to escape from the pressures of daily life?

The Five Star Yanglong Bay Mangrove

Tree Resort epitomizes the life of relaxation and exquisite taste of enjoyment.

(Bai Lan, 2018)

2.1.2.3   Tourism Public Signs and Notices

Tourist signs and notices are popular in public places. One may meet with them at roads, streets, hotels or even toilets. In *Random House Webster's Dictionary of American English* (1998), sign is "a board, placard, etc., with writing or a drawing on it that bears a warning, advertisement, or other information for public view." So Jin Huikang (2006) pointed out that tourist public signs were "the various languages used in public places." Harry Gray, Chairman of Geographical Signs, defined signs as "Signs are anything from a simplest way-finding or information 'marker' to the technically sophisticated communication of a message. Signing affects everybody—travelers, shoppers, visitors, drivers, etc., whether in the course of business or pleasure. Bad signing is at best irritating and at worst can be life threatening and dangerous." Public signs, together with pictures, are commonly found in transport and travel. They provide tourists with necessary information, publicize the tourist products (in advertisements), or even give a warning to the tourists. When the Olympic Game in 2008 was held, more public signs were put up to direct the foreign tourists. It is urgent to standardize the public signs in order to be favorable to the tourists.

English public signs can take a variety of forms: nouns, gerund, and verb phrases. They add to the novelty and vividness of the signs. Sometimes a warning is provided through the public signs.

Example 2-3　Wet Paint! 小心油漆
　　　　　　IN THE INTEREST OF THE PUBLIC
　　　　　　AND THE ENVIRONMENT
　　　　　　PLEASE
　　　　　　SWITCH OFF YOUR ENGINE
　　　　　　WHILST STATIONARY
　　　　　　为了公众利益和环境保护，机动车停驶时请关闭引擎。
　　　　　　TAXI RANK
　　　　　　PLEASE
　　　　　　QUEUE
　　　　　　THIS
　　　　　　SIDE
　　　　　　出租车站，请在此排队等候。

（http://www.bisu.edu.cn/e-signs/news_view.asp?id=12）

2.1.3　Functions of Tourism Text

The tourism text aims to introduce the cultures, histories and geography of the destination, arouse readers' interest and thus lead to the buying action. The forms it takes are very flexible: they may be published by the tourist bureau, travel agencies, or handed out in the streets. As a marketing tool, tourism text aims to spread the culture of the destination and promote the sales of tourist products. In *A Textbook of Translation*, based on Büler's three main functions of language, Newmark (2001) proposed that the three main functions of language were the expressive, informative and vocative functions. Among the three functions, vocative function is dominant because the target text focuses on the reactions of the readership, "calling upon the readership to act, think or feel, in fact to 'react' in the way intended by the text." On the basis of Newmark's model, the author summarizes the functions of tourism text as follows.

2.1.3.1   Informative Function

Informative function is one of the most important functions in tourism text. After World War II, the ever-increasing economy supplies people with disposable income and leisure time. More people begin to enjoy the privilege of traveling. They regard tourism as a means to experience the different culture and broaden their horizon. To arouse tourists' interest, good tourism text should contain detailed information of all kinds, such as culture, history, geography as well as fees, accommodation, telephone number and address. Especially for English tourism text, information is more important since westerners believe facts are more reliable than intuition and feelings. They seek helpful traveling information while neglecting the elegantly written text. This will be further discussed in the later chapters.

2.1.3.2   Vocative Function

Besides detailed information, good tourism text should be vocative. As mentioned before, vocative function spurs the readers to react in the same way intended by the source text. Readers' expectation to the tourism text shapes whether a future promotion will be achieved. In order to persuade the readers to act, publishers rack their brains to attract the readers. It is so often in tourism text that allusions, quotations, poetic lines, and other rhetoric devices are taking effects to impress the readers. Vocative function and informative function combine to improve the quality of the tourism text.

2.1.3.3   Aesthetic Function

Aesthetics is the cognition of beauty obtained by visual and aural organs. It mainly derives pleasure from seeing and listening, supplemented by smelling, tasting and touching. It is an advanced level of mental experience during which the combined image, emotion and cognition generate moral values. People long for tourism as a way of staying away from the fast tempo of life both physically and mentally. Reading tourist booklets can enrich their aesthetic experience as well as give guidance on the tourist destination. In tourism text, natural wonders like mountains, rivers, beaches amaze the readers; architecture, sculpture, battlefields, and ancient temples remind people of the past. Readers seem to wander in these places even though they don't go there on foot. Thus, the charming natural wonders and historical sites arouse interests in the tourists and elevate their aesthetic standards, leaving much fun to the readers. In addition, the rhythms of the language may enhance the euphony of the tourism text. Alliteration, assonance and consonance in the tourism text add up the vividness of the text.

2.1.3.4 Cultural Transmission

Culture refers to the total sum of material wealth and mental wealth generated by working people at a certain time. It includes habits, attitudes, beliefs, religions, customs, architecture, art, etc. High culture refers to literature, history, geography, education, science, drama, and music, while low culture denotes entertainment and everyday pleasure for the mass. One reason why tourists crowd into tourist destination is the abundant cultural relics. By 2003, China had 31 natural and cultural heritages in the World Heritage List, including the Great Wall, the Summer Palace, Mount Taishan and Confucius Temple, etc. Those cultural heritages inspire tourists to explore their histories. Tourism has become a cultural tour for the tourists to experience the social impact on the relics. However, pragmatic errors may arise when cross-cultural communication occurs. An American tourist will frown at it when talking about his/her families, salaries, and age while in China it is a common starting topic to break the ice. An effective way to avoid pragmatic errors is to read tourism texts which inform travelers of the etiquette to deal with local people. In this way, local culture is gradually accepted by the foreign travelers. Thus, foreign culture is blended into the local culture which promotes the cross-cultural communication.

All in all, four major functions play an active role in tourism text: informative, vocative, aesthetic function and cultural transmission. They don't work separately, but integrate with each other to render a good tourism text. Among the four, informative and vocative functions are the most important since they are elementary to make up for the tourism text. Aesthetic function and cultural transmission improve the readability of tourism text, making the reading process more enjoyable.

In addition, other functions are also displayed in the tourism text. Expressive function, for example, is manifested mostly in Chinese tourism text in that poems, allusions and couplets are usually employed by the Chinese writers to express their deep appreciation to the landscape.

2.2   A Review of Tourism Text Translation at Home and Abroad

2.2.1   Studies on Tourism Text Translation at Home

The study on tourism text is a comparatively new topic in China. With China's entry into WTO, the Olympic Games in 2008 and the World Exposition in Shanghai in 2010, more tourists have thronged into China. Tourism text, as a bridge to connect Chinese with foreigners, plays an increasingly positive role in cross-cultural communication. In recent years, more Chinese scholars have diverted their attention to tourism text translations in order to reduce the errors in the text and spread Chinese culture effectively to the outside world. Searching in CNKI with "tourism translation" as the key word, from the date of January 1st 2000 to January 1st 2021, it shows that articles in pictorials on tourism translation add up to 2, 533. The theses on tourism translation included 1 for doctor's degree and 822 for master's degree. In these published articles, the scholars put forward suggestions on tourism translation under the guidance of different translation theories. Their approaches can be summarized as follows.

2.2.1.1   Nida's Dynamic Equivalence Translation

Traditional translation researches focus on the translation of structures and grammars, or the relationship of source text to the target text in terms of either form or content. Nida made a breakthrough by proposing the theory of Dynamic Equivalence translation. He held that the reaction of target receptors to the target language text should be roughly equivalent to that of the original receptors to the original text. It is the similar reactions that lay foundation for the dynamic equivalence. Meanwhile, the expectations of the readers would determine the use of translation strategies in the translation process. Due to cultural differences, readers will have much difficulty in understanding the cultural-loaded words in tourism text. Especially in Chinese tourism text translation, the literal translation of poetic lines, allusions and quotations will puzzle the foreign readers. Translators could employ strategies like explication, footnoting, addition or omission to adapt the texts to the readers. Kang Ning (2005) pointed out the shared functions in Chinese and English tourism texts performed: directive, descriptive and informative functions. Among the three, the first was central to the tourism texts and its definition was applicable for both Chinese and English tourism texts. The other two played auxiliary roles and their definitions differed in the two languages. After that, Kang proposed that strategies for translating Chinese tourism texts into English should be based on three reader-centered principles: (a) striving to achieve adequate equivalence with the source text as far as the directive function is concerned; (b) making proper adjustment to the informational function of the source text in order to serve the target readers' need; (c) adapting the descriptive function of the source text to the target readers' aesthetic norms. Other scholars who study tourism translation in the perspective of dynamic equivalence include the following few. Wen Yue'e & Zhou Xiaoling(2005) and Wen Yue'e (2006) translated the brand names and Chinese menus under the guidance of functional equivalence. Chen Daiqiu (2005) specialized on translation of the cultural-loaded words and imagery in Chinese tourism texts. Those researchers all put the priority to the readers' reactions to the target text and attempt to supply ways to make up for the cultural loss.

2.2.1.2　Newmark's Communicative Translation

In *A Textbook of Translation*, Newmark (2001) held that all texts had three functions: expressive, informative and vocative functions. Tourism text is characterized by the vocative function, which "calls upon the readership to act, think or feel, in fact to 'react' in the way intended by the text." Based on the division of text types, he proposed two translation methods: communicative translation and semantic translation. Newmark (2001), in his book *Approaches to Translation*, defined the two terms as "Communicative translation attempts to produce on its readers an effect as close as possible to that obtained on the readers of the original. Semantic translation attempts to render, as closely as the semantic and syntactic structures of the second language allow, the exact contextual meaning of the original." In terms of tourism text, due to cultural differences, the translators have to adjust their versions to produce the same effects of the source texts on the target readers. The language in tourism text may be both informative and vocative, thus communicative translation is preferable to render the text clear and acceptable. Similarly, in tourism text the expressive function aims to elicit the readers' resonance. Quotations, like poetic and verse lines, and allusions, occur frequently to make the language vivid. Some of the quotations don't need to be translated, yet on other occasions these quotations are important since they'll widen readers' horizon and help tourists understand the Chinese culture. In this case, semantic translation is employed as a better way to achieve the effect. Ma Jinfeng (2003), in her MA thesis *Issues on Tourism Text*, pointed out that text materials aimed at providing information to readers in which semantic translation was required. On the other hand, the function of tourism text was to enlarge tourists' scope of knowledge, stimulate their interests, increase their delight during visits and publicize local culture of tourist destinations, so communicative translation method was often employed. She also listed some principles and techniques with compensations for untranslatability in translating Chinese tourism text into English. Zhang Dongxia (2006), based on Newmark's division of text type and reader response, put forward the translation of landscape description in Chinese tourism brochures.

2.2.1.3 Nord's Skopos Theory Translation

Skopos Theory was proposed by the German scholar Vermeer in the late 1970s, which served as the central theory of German functionalism. The word *skopos*, originated from Greek, is employed as the technical term for the translation purpose. Vermeer proposed that as a general rule it must be the intended purpose of the target text that played a decisive role in translation methods and strategies. From this point he defined the skopos rule: " Human is determined by its purpose, and therefore it is a function of its purpose." Nord (2001) believed that the skopos was largely constrained by the target readers and their situational and cultural background. In view of Vermeer, the source text was reconceptualized as an information offer, which the translator must interpret by selecting those features that most closely corresponded to the requirement of the target situation. Vermeer further summarized three possible kinds of purposes: the translator's general purpose (perhaps "to earn a living"); the communicative purpose of the target text (perhaps "to instruct the reader"); the purpose for a particular translation strategy or procedure (for example, "to translate literally in order to show the structural particularities of the source language"). In tourist writings, it usually refers to the second purpose: communicative purpose of the target text. Since the general purpose for tourism text is to arouse readers' interest in the tourist resources, positioning the intended target audience would offer the right translation strategies adopted in the situation. Li Yinan (2005) in her master thesis "A Study on C-E Translation of Tourist Writings" supplied strategies specially designed for Chinese to English translation such as prohibition on Chinglish, reader-oriented approach and manipulation of the source text. Reader-oriented approach was characterized by avoidance of technical terms and amplification of background information. Liu Liangxing (2006) believed good tourism translation would build a bridge over cultures under the framework of Skopos Theory. Kou Haishan (2010) classified four types of translation errors in the current tourism text translation: pragmatic, cultural, linguistic and text-specific errors. Then she pointed out the corresponding translation methods.

2.2.1.4　Semiotic Translation

Language is a system of signs. Semiotics as a research field dated back to Saussure. In his book *Course on General Linguistics*, Saussure pointed out that a sign referred to "something out there in the real world." "The linguistic sign does not unite a thing or a name, but a concept and a sound image." It is Saussure who laid the foundation of modern semiotics. American German scholar R. Carnap and American psychologist C. W. Morris furthered the theory of semiotics. Morris (1938) held that language as a sign system involved the triadic relationship among syntax, semantics and pragmatics. This triadic relationship corresponded to the sign's designative meaning, linguistic meaning and pragmatic meaning. An Chunping,

Zhang Zhizhong & Xing Zhaomei (2005), based on the division of three meanings, discussed their implications on translation from Chinese into English in tourist literature and its significance. Zhang Renxia (2004) took use of sociosemiotic approach to the translation of Chinese tourist literature. She believed that language as a semiotics had informative, expressive, vocative, aesthetic, phatic and meta-linguistic functions. She employed the semiotic concepts such as texts, contexts, tenor and social structure to analyze the translation in order to give thorough translation strategies to the text.

2.2.1.5   Cross-cultural Contrastive Analysis

Chen Gang (2004) defined that tourism translation was a cross-cultural, cross-psychological communication process. The Chinese language belongs to the Sino-Tibetan family whereas the English language is a branch of the Indo-European family. Their differences lie not only in the language forms, but also in the ways of thinking. The variances in people's habits, beliefs, religions, and customs in the cultural settings are reflected in language of the tourism texts. So many scholars conducted their researches from the perspectives of the cultural contrastive analysis. Yang Min & Ji Aimei (2003), with tourism texts randomly sampled from Shandong Province in China (QTT), and from America and Britain (ATT and BTT), analyzed the differences between Chinese and English tourism texts in terms of tenor, cultural schema, field and meta-message. It revealed that the Chinese original text of QTT was more formal than ATT and BTT, but its corresponding English version was less formal than them, and that ATT and BTT texts functioned mainly as a source of tourism information and advice while QTT texts were less relevant in this respect. Moreover, the cultural schema of QTT was distinct from that of ATT and BTT. Other scholars from the perspective of cross-cultural contrastive analysis include Liu Dejun (2006), Cao Dan (2005), Chen Wen (2005), Su Bing (2005), and Zhang Hui (2005).

Generally speaking, as cultural differences are the most striking features between tourism texts, the cross-cultural approach is widely accepted by scholars. According to the statistics of CNKI, articles about tourism translation from 2000 to 2020 in the perspective of cultural contrast amount to 376.

All the above approaches provide new insights into the tourism translation. Their strategies to tourism translation will undoubtedly improve the translation quality and therefore elevate the image of tourist destination. However, lacking of uniform guidance of translation theory, the strategies to tourism text translation seem to be far from systematic and need to be tested whether they are applicable to the local culture. That is why the author employs the Adaptation Theory in tourism translation.

2.2.2　Studies on Tourism Text Translation Abroad

Tourism text is a genre which focuses on the reactions of the target readers. Scholars from abroad carried out their researches on tourism text from different perspectives.

By evaluating an English translation of a German tourist booklet, House (1981) proposed a model for translation quality assessment based on Halliday's Systemic Functional Grammar. She then proposed the translation strategies of covert translation and overt translation. Covert translation was defined as a "translation which enjoyed the status of an original ST (source text) in the target culture." House adopted a functional equivalence approach to translation and believed that the notion of "covert translation" embodied the ideal case of this translation theory: the achievement of functional equivalence. She also pointed out some of the difficulties in evaluating the booklet. When comparing the version with the original manuscript, there were differences among the functional parameters of "social role relationship." By leaving the italicized information implicit, the German brochure had a special effect on the audience: people were cultured enough to know who Hans Sachs was and what "Männleinlaufen" and the "Englische Gruss" referred to while the literal English translation lost this effect. In her evaluation, she didn't treat these differences as errors but as adaptations to the different sociocultural background of the target readers.

Gutt (2004) furthered House's study on functional equivalence translation by considering another tourist brochure that illustrated these points still more clearly. The texts were taken from a brochure provided for passengers on board the Funnjet car ferry operating between Travemünde and Helsinki. Side by side on one page it had two write-ups that gave information about the ferry, with all its technical advantages and the route. In spite of some shared parallel structure and information, there were very clear differences between the versions. In Gutt's opinion, how to deal with these differences was a functional equivalence translation matter. However, he also pointed out that formulating a general translation theory of functional equivalence that was explicit, coherent and accommodated all the discussed differences seemed a formidable task indeed.

Another two figures on tourism translation are Rosa Lore's Sanz and Eric Castello. Rosa published an article: "the Translation of Tourism Literature," which analyzed the connectors in thematic position in English translation of Spanish tourism literature. She compared texts originally written in English with the translated English versions from Spanish source texts. She postulated that the analysis of the patterns of theme selection provided important insights into the translation of a specific genre.

Castello (2002) adopted a systematic-functional approach to describe the language and its structure in tourism text by means of corpus linguistics.

Gandin (2013) carried out corpus-based studies on the tourism translation from a variety of languages into English. His analysis identified the potential differences in the discursive patterns and stylistic features in the tourism translation versions compared with tourism texts originally written in English. He found that by employing translation strategies such as simplification, explicitation, normalization, interference and even leveling out tendencies, the translated tourism texts differed from the original ones in the discursive patterns and stylistic features. Therefore, the typical patterns and verbal techniques were often employed in terms of frequency and discursive patterns in tourism text translation.

2.3   A Review of Adaptation Theory

Translation is a complicated conversion process from the source language to the target language, which involves the interrelation of sender, translator and receiver. Different translators proposed different translation strategies from various perspectives. The dichotomies of literal and free translation, domestication and alienation, covert and overt translation touch on different angles of translation. However, variation in translation strategies will make the evaluation of translation hard to proceed. Besides, some of the translation principles are not so systematic for translators to follow. Belgium pragmatist Jef. Verschueren proposed the Adaptation Theory in 1999. He held that language had three characteristics: variability, negotiability and adaptability. In order to account for the language phenomenon, one must consider four aspects: contextual correlates of adaptability, structural objects of adaptability, dynamics of acceptability and salience of adaptation process. This panoramic perspective covers the macropragmatic issues like language, code and tenor as well as the micropragmatic issues like the syntax, therefore proves great vitality in explaining language phenomenon including discourse markers and code-switching.

Since the Adaptation Theory is comprehensive, scholars show great interest in it. Wu Yaxin (2003) analyzed the discourse markers in conversation controlled by metapragmatic awareness. She argued that using discourse markers could emphasize the statement, express ideas on the statement, confirm the content and initiate or end a topic. Li Chengtuan (2006) revisited the pragmatic functions of interrogative forms with examples of questions in TV feature interviews. Yang Qing (2006) analyzed the structural metaphor as realization of adaptability and its functioning in Chinese TV talk shows.

Other research topics under the framework of Adaptation Theory are on the fuzziness on news language (Zhang Junyi, 2008), Chinese irony (Qin Haitao, 2006), advertisement (Li Yan, 2006; Zhang Yanmin, 2006), teaching of reading comprehension (Zhang Jinrong, 2006), interpretation (Xia Cui, 2005), social deixis (Li Xiaoguang, 2005), repetition (Peng Juan, 2005), responding in Chinese court-room setting (Liu Ping, 2003), translation strategies on tourism texts (Yan Fengxia, 2007; Zhou Qian, 2011) and so on.

The Adaptation Theory also sheds light on translation. Zeng Wenxiong

(2002, 2003) postulated that in interpretive process translators should adapt to the content, language structure of the source language and the dynamic process of the interpretation. Ge Lingling (2002) showed that the contextual adaptation determined the word choice and word meaning in translation. She furthered the research on the adaptation to target language. In her views, the reconstruction of the target text was translator's dynamic adaptation to the context and language structure of the source text during which communicator's salience and real purpose would be revealed.

Song Zhiping (2004) found the translation process was manifested in the choice of the text, cultural viewpoint, meaning of text and procession of information. The choices were influenced by the setting, aesthetics, and acceptance of the target readers. Gao Yun & Han Li (2004) made use of the dynamic contextual Adaptation Theory to account for the connotation of the source text. Yan Minfen (2002) provided a new way in poem translation by translating metaphors in poems.

In recent years, the study on translation under the guidance of Adaptation Theory has become a hot topic. Gao Hui (2004) carried out his researches on the advertisement translation from the perspective of contextual adaptation. Zeng Wenxiong (2006) employed cultural adaptation in a pragmatic perspective to appreciate aesthetics in translation. He believed that cultural pragmatics could explain the translation of language structure, mental world, social world, physical world and cultural world.

Bai Lan (2018) illustrated adaptation to translation of the Chinese language and culture from Chinese to English tourism text materials. She believed that in Chinese to English text translation, adaptation should be applied not only to the target culture but also to the Chinese original text. Under the background of traditional Chinese culture going abroad, translators need to be politically sensitive, highlight multiculturalism by preserving the specialty of Chinese culture and translate the Chinese text materials into English accurately with the correct word choice.

To sum up, ever since the introduction of Adaptation Theory in 1999, it has aroused the scholars' interest in different fields. As a thorough and systematic theory, the Adaptation Theory has great implications in relevant fields such as teaching, translation and linguistics, to name just a few. In terms of translation, as mentioned above, it has shown great vitality in advertisement translation, literary translation, poem translation and interpretation. However, relevant translation studies on tourism text materials are relatively few. That is the reason why the author takes up the Adaptation Theory to analyze the tourism text.

2.4 Problems of Current Tourism Text Translation

Tourism text translation has been a hot topic in recent years. The roaring tourism industry attracts more scholars' attention on this newly developed industry. However, the corresponding translation of tourism text couldn't catch up with the tide. Some translation mistakes are so frequently found that they hamper the cross-cultural communication and damage the image of the destination. Wen Jun et al. (2002) summarized six kinds of translation mistakes in tourism text translation: spelling mistakes, grammatical mistakes, chinglish, misuse of words, tautology and cultural misunderstandings. Even though many scholars carry out a large sum of researches on the mistakes of tourism text translation, errors still pop up in all kinds of tourism texts. In order to solve this problem, the author categories the mistakes in the present tourism text translation as follows: grammatical mistakes, pragmatic mistakes and cultural mistakes.

2.4.1 Grammatical Mistakes

Lacking of standardization and corresponding publication regulations and laws, mistakes in translation of tourism text create barriers to cross-cultural communication. Grammatical mistakes are the most common mistakes in the tourism text. They are exemplified in spelling mistakes and syntactic mistakes.

2.4.1.1 Spelling Mistakes

Spelling mistakes are the misspelling of words usually made by the writer's carelessness or for press mistakes. Once the author visited Dai Temple at the foot of Mount Taishan in Shandong Province, the grandeur of Dai Temple left an unforgettable impression on her except for a few mistakes. On the wall of the hall hang a big notice, "Reserve the environment." Here *reserve* as a verb originally means to keep or store something for future use, while the notice actually means to request the tourists to protect the environment in case of being destroyed. Thus, *reserve* should be replaced by *preserve* with a letter "p" adding in front of it. Maybe the letter was missed due to the storm, but such wrong spelling mistakes would easily be laughed at by the foreign tourists if not properly handled.

2.4.1.2   Syntactic Mistakes

The ordering of sentences without grammatical guidance will lead to syntactic mistakes. This demands that a translator must be competent at two languages, at least in grammar. The below text is coined from http://www.dzwww.com on Mount Taishan.

Example 2-4   The history of Mount Taishan can dating back to the provenance of Chinese culture and early in Chunqiu Period, Mount Taishan had been reserved for imperial sacrifices to Heaven, leading to its current paramount situation.

This paragraph consists of a complete sentence with four branching sentences. The obvious mistake lies in the phrase "can dating back" where "can" is a modal verb which needs to be accompanied by an original verb form. However, readers are still at a loss after the revision. The tricky point is in the phrase "and early in the Chunqiu Period." As an adverbial phrase of time, is it an apposition of "the provenance of Chinese culture" or a pre-modification for "Mount Taishan to be reserved for imperial sacrifices to Heaven"? Taking the whole context into account, we arrive at the conclusion that the phrase belongs to the latter. In addition, since there is only one sentence in the paragraph, as for the present participle "leading," will it modify the verb "date" or the phrase "had been reserved?" In order to disambiguate the sentence, the author revises it as follows.

Revised: The history of Mount Taishan can date back to the provenance of

Chinese culture. And early in the Spring and Warring Period, Mount Taishan had been reserved for imperial sacrifices to Heaven, leading to its current paramount situation.

2.4.2 Pragmatic Mistakes

Pragmatic mistakes are committed during language use in communication. As translation is a complicated process involving the linguistic, cultural and social variances between the two nations, pragmatic mistakes may take place and misunderstandings arise.

Example 2-5   ST: 金茂大厦
              TT1: Jin Mao Building
              TT2: Jin Mao Tower

(Weng Fengxiang, 2002)

Situated in the downtown area of Shanghai, this building promotes commercial and cultural exchange. It is shaped like a tower with eight angles on all the sides. TT1 is a literal translation of the source in which "building" only signifies it is an architecture without any specialties. In TT2, the translator presented to the readers the spectacular shape of the building, adding much vividness to the text. No wonder the tourists would recognize the tower at the sight of all the buildings. Another similar pragmatic mistake is shown below.

Example 2-6   ST: 教师休息室
              TT1: Teachers' Restroom
              TT2: Teachers' Resting Room / Teachers' Retiring Room

Restroom in the English-speaking countries is a euphemism for toilet, and in Canada, people usually call it "bathroom." When talking about human organs, sex or death, etc., English people usually mention them in a round-about way. "Teachers' Restroom" here denotes it is a toilet especially designed for teachers, but what the source text intends to inform us is that this place is in fact a resting place for teachers. The translator translated the source text literally while neglecting the social customs of the target country. It would be better rendered as "Teachers' Resting Room" or "Teachers' Retiring Room.""

Example 2-7   ST: 大明湖历史悠久，景色优美，名胜古迹周匝其间。尤其他乃繁华都市之中的天然湖泊，实属难得。

TT: Daming Lake has a long history, and it has beautiful scenery, with scenic spots and historical sites in between. Especially, it is a natural lake in the prosperous city, which is really <u>one in a thousand.</u>

(Information Office of Jinan Municipal People's Government, 2005)

"One in a thousand" metaphorically connotes the rareness of the lake compared with others. In the target text, it is used as a non-attributive clause to comment on the "natural lake in the prosperous city." It is a common practice for Chinese to give a comment after a list of facts. Yet in English, commenting words are seldom put at the end of a sentence. The sentence balance is damaged as a result of the conversion of orders. Combined with other mistakes in the target text, the author corrects them as follows.

Revised: Daming Lake boasts a long history and beautiful scenery with scenic spots and historical sites around the lake. Especially, it is reputed as one in a thousand for a natural lake in the prosperous city.

2.4.3   Cultural Mistakes

Tourism text aims at offering necessary tourism information to the future tourists and most important of all, spreading culture to the foreign tourists. However, some translations neglect the cultural connotation that tourism text conveys, thus create misunderstandings among the foreigners. Those mistakes hamper the cross-cultural communication between China and foreign countries. Efforts should be made to improve the situation in tourism text translation.

Example 2-8   ST: 虎跑泉

TT1: The Dreamed Tiger Running Spring

TT2: Tiger Spring

(Chen Gang, 2004)

In one of the booklets introducing Hangzhou, this famous scenic spot is literally translated. In fact, there is a story behind the spring. Legend has it that in AD819 of the Tang dynasty, after traveling a lot of places, a monk wanted to have a rest in this place. Lacking water, he prepared to move out. On the night, he dreamed of a fairy who told him two tigers were summoned up to dig out a well. The next day, he woke up only to see the spring, hence the spring got the name. Therefore, " 跑 " in the source text does not literally mean running, but a homophone with " 刨 " (which means to dig up something with feet). This scenic spot should be translated as "The Dreamed Tiger Pawed Spring," or shortened as "Tiger Spring." Other similar mistakes are shown in the following.

Example 2-9   ST: 寒山寺

TT1: Cold Mountain Temple

TT2: Han Shan Temple

Many Chinese people are familiar with this temple since the Chinese poet Zhang Ji in the Tang dynasty once wrote, " 姑苏城外寒山寺，夜半钟声到客船。 " (Beyond the city walls, from Temple of Cold Hill; Bells break the ship-borne roamer's dream and midnight still—translated by Xu Yuanchong). In fact, the temple is named after a monk called Han Shan who once lived in the temple. If translated freely, the cultural connotation in the temple will be reduced by a large amount. Therefore, the name of the monk is added in the second version to inform tourists of the story behind it.

To avoid cultural mistakes, translators need not only to master the grammatical knowledge, but also to foster the cross-cultural awareness. Comprehensive awareness on the destination's customs, social habits, beliefs and religions are elementary to make a successful translator. Nida (2004) said, "A translator must engage in thousands of decisions involving both selection and arrangement to fit another culture, a different language, diverse editors and publishers, and finally a reading audience." In Jinan of Shandong Province, there is a famous scenic spot comprising 26 springs called " 五龙潭 "(literally translated as "Five-Dragon Pool"). Chinese legend has it that the pool was too deep to be fathomable in the old days.

Each time when the drought came by, people prayed to the Pool for rain and then came the rain. In memory of the Pool, people enshrined five statues of Dragon God (In Chinese culture, a dragon god is in charge of rain) to worship them. Furthermore, dragon in Chinese context is a symbol of high social status endowed with supreme power. Chinese kings are regarded as the sons of dragon god to rule over the mass whose clothes, walls, roofs, and even bedrooms in the palaces are decorated with dragons in different shapes to symbolize the supreme power. By contrast, dragon in foreign legends is a big and fierce monster that can spray out fires. In English literature, it is a symbol of evil as in the Bible, "And the great dragon was cast out, that old serpent, called the Devil, and Satan, which receiveth the whole world." Undoubtedly, the literal translation of "Five-Dragon Pool" may frighten the foreign tourists without any Chinese cultural background information. The author then translated it as "Wu Long Pool or Five-Tiger Pool." According to the statistics of the questionnaire conducted by the author (readers may refer to Chapter Three), 60% of the non-English major postgraduates and 30% of the English-major postgraduates agree with a transliteration "Wu Long Pool."

In conclusion, the author summarizes three kind of mistakes frequently found in tourism text translation: grammatical mistakes, pragmatic mistakes and cultural mistakes. Grammatical mistakes are avoidable after a comprehensive study on the target language grammar. Pragmatic and cultural mistakes are the advanced mistakes in which social, cultural and psychological factors are involved to put a higher demand on the translators. Therefore, it is necessary for translators to enrich their horizon and read widely on the culture of the destination. To be specific, in tourism text translation, translators should be at first competent at two languages and then get to know the geography, history, economics and political development of the destination. Last but not least, as tourism translators, they'd better have professional knowledge on tourism, like tourism products, travel economics, management, marketing and tourism planning, which contributes to the preciseness and appropriateness of translation. In a word, a translator is not only a translator, but also a cultural disseminator.

Tourism text, as both an informative and vocative text, conveys information of the destination and passes down culture between different nations. Translation on the tourism text is of vital importance since it takes on the responsibility of information conveyance and cultural transmission to the foreigners. However, with no uniform translation briefs and corresponding regulations, the standard of tourism text translation varies and can't meet with the demands of swarming tourists. The flourishing tourist industry is calling upon the rapid improvement of tourism text translation. Under such circumstances, the author proposes her model on tourism text translation under the framework of the Adaptation Theory. This model will enjoy the privilege of theoretical and pragmatic significance to the future studies.

Chapter 3
Theoretical Framework

Pragmatics is the study of language use in human communication confined by the conditions of society. This term was firstly proposed by American philosopher Charles Morris in the 1930s who defined pragmatics as the study of the relationship between signs and their interpreters. However, it was neglected as a waste basket for picking up the researches that other disciplines cast away with. Not until between the 1970s and 1980s had pragmatics been established as a branch of subject. As a new subject with great vitality, pragmatics develops systematically and forms a series of new concepts of its own: deixis, speech act theory, cooperative principles, politeness principle and relevance theory, to name just a few. These theories have proved great explanatory force in linguistics, literature and translation. With the deepening study on pragmatics, the division of pragmatics has been more specified. Trans-cultural pragmatics, interlingual pragmatics, societal pragmatics and cognitive pragmatics promote the flourishing of modern pragmatics.

Traditional pragmatists view pragmatics as a separate branch of linguistics, as phonology, phonetics, semantics, syntax and discourse analysis do. It has its own technical terms such as presupposition, deixis, and speech act theory. Though specific, those separate researches couldn't encompass the thorough characteristics of pragmatic studies. This problem was not solved until Belgium pragmatist Jef. Verschueren proposed the Adaptation Theory, a comprehensive pragmatic perspective in 1999. In his book *Understanding Pragmatics*, Verschueren postulated that pragmatics had involved in cognitive, social, and cultural perspectives on linguistic phenomena in relation to their usage in forms of behavior.

3.1 Adaptation Theory

3.1.1 Making Choices

Verschueren's theory was enlightened from Darwin's evolutionary theory. Darwin in his 1859 book of *Origin of Species* argued the evolution of organism would experience three periods of variation species, survival adaptation and species evolution. Among them, the survival adaptation was the commonest to species as a result of survival of the fittest. The evolutionary epistemology extended the biological theory, and especially its natural selection paradigm, to all aspects of behavior and social culture, including language, learning and science. Evolutionary epistemology regarded evolution as the process of acquiring new knowledge. Verschueren (2000) pointed out when it came to language, the viability of such functional explanations may depend on the distinction between natural selection mechanism in evolution and reinforcement mechanisms, the latter being closer to what seems to happen in the shaping of languages and by extension, in the functioning of language. Based on this, Verschueren believed that language also shared the characteristics of natural selection. He argued that languages consisted of continuously making linguistic choices, consciously or unconsciously, for language-internal (i.e. structural) or language-external reasons. Language-internal denoted the linguistic property of language, such as phonetics, semantics, and syntax while language-external involved the cultural and social parameters. According to Verschueren (2000), the choices we make in languages should be noted from the following perspectives.

Firstly, we make choices at different levels of language structures. Based on the context, the genre should be foremost selected in order to identify the speakers' general purpose. Then the speakers choose the sentence structures where certain grammatical forms are embedded. In terms of speaking, intonation patterns and structures are picked up because occasionally they may confine the usage of certain genres. It should be noted that the choices we made at different language levels are concurrent. Secondly, language strategies are chosen in order to meet the speakers' communication purpose. For instance, the style, terms of address and the voices could be flexibly employed. Thirdly, the choices occur both in the interpretation and production process of speaking, thus equal attention should be given to the two types of choice-making. Fourthly, choices must be made no matter consciously or unconsciously. When using language, the speaker should make choices even though he can't achieve the communication purpose on the spot. Lastly, the choices we made give rise to other alternatives in the different context. Different word choices may reflect the speakers' different ideology.

Translation is a process of consciously making choices. It is a complicated code-switching process which accounts for the conversion of micropragmatic aspects like phonology, phonetics, semantics and syntax as well as macropragmatic aspects such as language variety, style and cultural element. A translator faces a variety of choices during the translation performance. Before translation gets started, a translator searches for the background information to ensure: (1) which language forms should be used, formal or informal, plain or vivid; (2) what types of text it belongs to: informative, expressive or vocative, so as to choose the right translation strategies; (3) the cultural standpoint. As a mediator between two cultures, a translator meets with the dilemma of cultural penetration from foreign culture to the native culture. Choosing a right cultural standpoint will determine what translation strategies should be taken up. The struggle between foreignization and domestication in translation studies in recent years is a case in point.

During the translation process, among dozens of synonyms in language, translators select the right word according to the different layers of language including phonetics, semantics, syntax and the discourse. Besides, translators should read between the lines to get the connotation of cultural and social meaning embedded in the text. Making a wise choice of these elements will add up the idiomatic and pragmatic value of the versions.

3.1.2 Three Key Notions in Adaptation Theory

As choice-making is inevitable and permeates every level of language use, we should bear in mind how the paradigm works. Three hierarchically related notions are served to illustrate the process of language use: variability, negotiability and adaptability.

According to Verschueren (2000), variability is "the property of language which defines the range of possibilities from which choices can be made."

Negotiability is "the property of language responsible for the fact that choices are not made mechanically or confined to strict rules or fixed from form-function relationships, but rather on the basis of highly flexible principles and strategies."

Adaptability is "the property of language which enables human beings to make negotiable linguistic choices from a variable range of possibilities in such a way as to approach points of satisfaction for communicative needs."

The three notions are inseparable. Variability and negotiability lay the foundation for adaptability which finally achieves the aim of language use. Variability and negotiability provide possibility and means where adaptation process occurs to guarantee the ongoing of communication process. Among them, adaptability is primarily important since it is both the means and ends for successful communication. Translation shares the distinct features of adaptability. On one hand, translation works for a special purpose in the same way as language works for successful communication. Nord (2001) once said, "The prime principle determining any translation process is the purpose (Skopos) of the overall translation action." Translation of literary works is to enhance the aesthetics as well as provide moral lessons to the readers; translation of technical articles is to introduce new invention and technologies abroad to develop the home productivity; practical translation serves for the reality whose contents will be popular and needy enough to put into use once translated. Tourism translation, advertisement translation and contract translation belong to this category. In accordance with divergent translation briefs, translators make adjustments to adapt to the stylistic requirements of different texts. The adaptations range from macrolevel like discourse, style and code to microlevel like sound, word choice and syntax.

On the other hand, translators make passive and active adaptation to the source text. Passive adaptation refers to adaptation to the cultural elements and social norms in beliefs, customs, values and social settings. They are "out there," so translators adjust their mind to suit for the target readers' cultural and social context. Active adaptation involves translators' active roles in choosing sound, words and syntax in order to suit with the target language. In this case, translators have the final say in selecting these items based on different translation briefs.

Example 3-1   Oh! She is the most beautiful creature I ever beheld. (*Pride and Prejudice*, by Jane Austin)

(Wang Jianguo, 2005)

According to the statistics by Wang Xiaoyuan (2002), the translation of "the most beautiful creature" in Chinese includes 10 versions: "这么美丽的一个尤物、这么美丽的尤物、绝色美人儿、绝色美人、最美的人儿、最漂亮的女子、最美丽的姑娘、最漂亮的姑娘、我所见过的姑娘数她长得最美、这么美丽的小姐 ." These various Chinese equivalences clarify the translator's active manipulation on word choices which improves the version's vividness and readability.

In addition, translators should adapt to the target readers' feedback. Translating process is cross-cultural communication during which new culture will filter and be gradually accepted by the native speakers. Therefore, the target readers' feedback to the source text is vitally important to testify the quality of the versions. Nida once held that relation of target receptors to the target text should be roughly equivalent to the relationship between the original receptors to the original text. An elegant translation abundant in cultural allusions in the Chinese source text can't be fully acknowledged by the target English readers for lack of background knowledge. During translation process, translators should take the target readers' physical, cultural, cognitive and linguistic factors into account and adjust their mind to the target readers when contradiction occurs. Furthermore, dozens of translation versions of the same source text could be left to the native speakers to decide which version will suit best the readers' language and cultural habits. The widely accepted version by the readers will enjoy the highest rank of translation. The competition between different versions will surely promote the flourishing of translation studies. The other side of the coin is that the result of competition, survival of the fittest, is just an illustration of Adaptation Theory by itself.

3.1.3　Four Angles of Investigation

Using adaptability as a starting point, four angles of investigation should be taken into account when a linguistic phenomenon is approached pragmatically: contextual correlates of adaptability, structural objects of adaptability, the dynamics of adaptability and the salience of adaptation process.

3.1.3.1　Contextual Correlates of Adaptability

Verschueren (2000) defined contextual correlates of adaptability as "all the ingredients of the communicative context with which linguistic choices have to be inter-adaptable. The range goes from aspects of the physical surroundings (e.g. distance as an influence or loudness of voice) to social relationships between speakers and hearers and aspects of the interlocutors' state of mind." Context is not simply "out there," but is subject to negotiation and variation in communication with the speech event in relation to which they can be seen to function. Context can be divided into communicative context and linguistic context. Linguistic context is realized through cohesion, intertextuality and sequencing. Proper handling of linguistic context in translation will enhance the coherence and unity in the target text. Because of the limited space, this will be discussed in the next chapter. Communicative context comprises physical world, mental world and social world. In combination with translation studies, the communicative context can be specified as follows.

3.1.3.1.1　Physical World

The physical world is comprised of temporal deixis and spatial deixis. Temporal deixis refers to the event time, time of utterance and reference time. Spatial reference may take the form of absolute spatial relations like North, South, East and West. Or it is relative to a certain location, namely either utterer space or reference space. Pairs of concepts like "left" and "right", "here" and "there", or the time phrase "10 o'clock" are used to indicate direction, typically requiring the spatial orientation of the utterer. Besides, communicator's body postures, gestures, gaze and physical appearance as well as physical conditions are connected with choices in uttering and interpreting. Certain material conditions should also be included in the physical world to lay the material foundation for successful communication. In translation, translators must pay special attention to the differences and make adaptations when dealing with the two cultures. For example, in expressing the locations, " 东北 " in Chinese (literally mean east and north) becomes "northeast" in English. The distinctions of deixis can be better illustrated in the temporal reference in the following examples:

Example 3-2   ST: But we are getting <u>ahead</u> of the story.
              TT: 可是我们已经说到故事的<u>后面</u>去了。

(Bao Huinan, 2001)

"Ahead" in English means something to happen in the future. For instance, the phrase "Go ahead!" is a request for the speaker to keep going the conversation. By contrast in Chinese, " 前 " (literally means ahead) denotes the past events while " 后 " (literally means behind) refers to the future events. Chinese poet Chen Zi'ang in the Tang dynasty once wrote a poem, " 前不见古人，后不见来者。念天地之悠悠，独怆然而涕下。" Chen in his poem sentimentally expressed loneliness and regrets for not achieving his ambition when viewing from the pavilion. " 前 " and " 后 " here denoted the passing time and the future time respectively. In Example 3-2, "ahead of the story" shows that "we" are talking so fast to reach the next part of the story before one could realize it. Hence, a Chinese equivalent " 后 " is offered to demonstrate the fast speed of our talking.

3.1.3.1.2   Social World

Social world refers to the norms and principles abided by the communicators through social settings and institutions. The utmost relationships observed between linguistic choices and the social world are the setting, institution, or community in communicative norms. Due to differences in cultural traditions, customs and habits, Chinese vary greatly in social norms and etiquette from the foreigners. Therefore, translators should be culturally sensitive to reflect the cultural connotation in the text. Once a Chinese host invited foreign friends to have dinner at home. When the dinner was served, the host toasted like this:

Example 3-3   ST: 今天饭菜不好，请多包涵。来，先干上一杯。

TT1: Forgive me for the food today is not well served. Now, to everyone, cheers!

TT2: They are best dishes we're able to prepare. Please make yourself at home. Now, to every one, cheers!

(Bao Huinan & Bao Ang, 2004)

TT1 is a literal translation of the source text. In Chinese context, people often use expressions like "not so good," "just so so" to show modesty even though they have done their best to prepare the dishes. However, Americans regard their achievements and others' praise as an affirmation to their ability, so they love to show their friends how good they are. Besides, as most Americans are frank, they regard the host's words as insincere and hypocritical. Why don't they offer the best food to the guests? Are they acting on purpose? Thus, TT2 adapts to the social customs by making the changes "the best dishes we are able to prepare."

3.1.3.1.3   Mental World

Mental world activated in language use contains cognitive and emotive elements. While cognitive elements conceptualize the mental and social world where social interaction is interpreted, the emotive elements provide the attitudinal conditions for pertaining and coloring interaction. Adaptation to the readers' mental world in translation contributes to comprehend the tourists' cognition.

Example 3-4   ST: （赵辛楣）一肚皮的酒，几乎全化成酸醋……（Qian Zhongshu, 1991）

TT: The wine in Xinmei's stomach turned to sour vinegar in his jealousy.

Vinegar in Chinese setting not only denotes a sauce, but also metaphorically connotes the envies and jealousies when finding the beloved one stays with another boy/girl. The sentence "The wine... turns into vinegar." in the source text implies how jealous Xinmei is. However, this would confuse the foreigners as vinegar in the foreign countries is just a sauce to cook delicious food. Therefore, the translator adds "in his jealousy" to make the readers aware of the mental changes in Zhao Xinmei. Physical world, mental world and social world are interrelated to affect language users' word choices in producing and interpreting utterances.

The utterer and interpreter are considered as the focal points, since the contextual aspects of the physical, social and mental worlds do not give a full play until they have been activated by language users' cognitive process. Interpreters adapt to the three worlds of the utterers through the linguistic context. The dotted lines are lines of vision, all of which function as a correlate of adaptability. This can be illustrated in Figure 3-1.

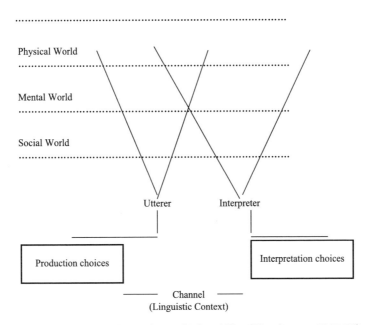

Figure 3-1   Contextual Correlates of Adaptability（Verschueren, 2000:76）

3.1.3.2   Structural Objects of Adaptability

Since the communicative choices occur at every plane of linguistic structure, pragmatic phenomena can be related to any layer of structure, from phoneme, word, syntax to discourse. Adaptation to structural objects can be choices among languages, codes and styles; utterance-building ingredients; utterance and utterance clusters and lastly utterance-building principles. In translation, a text with appropriate adaptability to the target text's structure will be more idiomatic.

3.1.3.3　Dynamics of Adaptability

The generation of meaning is not stable, but dynamic adaptation to the structural, physical, mental and social worlds. By "adaptation," attention should be paid to the changing communication strategies when negotiating the choices of production and interpretation. These can be manifested in relation to time, context and language structure. As a key point in Adaptation Theory, dynamics has great implications on translation.

The first is the dynamic translation on time. A source text is a product of particular setting. With time passing by, an old translation to the source text may not be fit for the social context of present people. The Bible translation in Renaissance was once regarded as magnificent classics at that time, but as time goes by, new versions of the Bible translation line up as a result of the changing social settings and aesthetic values.

The second is the dynamic translation on context. Rojo (1994) proposed that dynamics of conversational interaction should be constructed on the basis of the conflicting tendencies towards the preservation of privacy and the formation of alliances. This would be manifested in terms of social relationships. As communication took place during the social interactions, communicators adapted their personal needs to the social norms so as to select the needy information, whether explicit meaning or implicit meaning, the occasions to use the appropriate words, the interplay between positive face and negative face and between power and policy. Besides, personal knowledge, beliefs and meaning intentions affected the adaptability in the communication process.

From the perspective of translation, in order to suit a particular context, translators adapt to the target readers' social and mental needs by making alterations whenever necessary. Lu Xun's diversion on translation of Science Fiction is an explication of dynamic adaptability to the social context.

The third is the dynamic translation on structure. Language progresses through a chronological order—a linearity which accounts for the ordering of communication, or the timing of backchannel cues in conversation, the switching between codes and the entire turn-taking system and repairs, etc. Linearity determines the proper ordering in sentential (like word order) as well as suprasentential levels. In actual communication, linearity is not strictly observed because utterers and interpreters changed the content of conversation to meet with the communicative needs. In the microlanguage level, translators change the word choice to lay emphasis or leave a deeper impression on the readers. In the macrolanguage level, when the source text is not written logically, translators have the responsibility to adjust the sentence order to make the text more coherent. These techniques are often employed in translation of discourse which reflects the dynamic adaptation to the overall source text.

3.1.3.4　Salience of the Adaptation Process

Verschueren (2000) held that all dynamic aspects of language use, which could be situated in terms of structurally identifiable choices and contextual properties, were processed through the medium of adaptability-salience. Chances were that every linguistic behavior could be dominated by the consciousness. The choices making in general combined with the contributing mental processes were influenced by the different degrees of salience. Social norms, together with individual knowledge, shaped the formulation of communicator's choice-making. Therefore, adaptive strategies to the social salience would guarantee the ongoing communication. Salience undertook by the communicators to self-monitor the language they are using is called metapragmatic awareness. According to Verschueren, it is a "systematic study of the metalevel, where indicators of reflexive awareness are to be found in the actual choice-making that constitutes language use." Metapragmatic awareness can be better illustrated by the use of discourse markers. Discourse markers could express the speaker's initiation of a new topic, hesitation to make a decision or turn-taking in a conversation. Hence, translation of discourse markers should express the implicit meaning that is embedded in the sentence.

Example 3-4　ST: Jeanne: Oh, come, Mathilde, surely you can tell an old friend.

Mathilde: Well…well, it was because of that necklace.

TT: 珍妮：快说吧，对老朋友还用隐瞒吗？

玛蒂尔德：……都是因为那条项链。

(Ma Xiao, 2003)

This conversation is extracted from the French writer Maupassant's *The Necklace*. Mathilde borrowed a necklace from her friend Jeanne to match her new dress in the evening party but unfortunately lost it. She worked for ten years to pay off the debts only to find the necklace was a fake one. The discourse marker "well" reflected Mathilde's hesitation to tell her friend the truth since it was a humiliating experience. The translator adapted Mathilde's mental world by use of suspension points. As the saying goes, "Silence is golden." Silence could express the speakers' embarrassment, hesitation or disagreement. It seems that all the sufferings and tortures that Mathilde had experienced in the past ten years are embedded in the suspension points.

These four aspects of adaptability are not only complementary, but also carry different functional loads under the pragmatic perspective. Their interrelationships can be demonstrated in Figure 3-2.

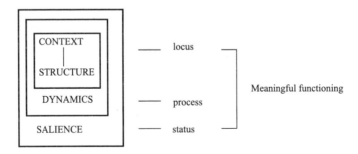

Figure 3-2   Interplay of Four Aspects in Adaptability (Verschueren, 2000: 67)

First, the contextual correlates and structural objects can be combined to define the locus of adaptation because they contain the linguistic and extra-linguistic coordinates in the speech event. Their relationship is the most important because it provides a starting point for specific descriptive tasks in pragmatics and as parameters throughout the investigation.

Second, dynamics permeates the interrelationship of context and structure in a certain process. It cares for the nature and development of the relationship between context and structure. That is to say, processes are the dynamics of context-structure interrelationships. Hence dynamics is put into a box containing context and structure.

Third, the dynamics of interrelationship between structure and context are conducted under the salience of the speakers' mind. Hence an investigation of the salience of adaptation processes will clarify the status in the consciousness of human mind. The process is of vital importance since metapragmatic awareness is generated under this framework.

Fourth, the superordinate concern which regards pragmatic studies as dynamic processes operating on context-structure at different planes of salience contributes to understand the meaningful functioning of language and identify the dynamic generation of meaning in use.

The four angles of investigation have great implications in accounting for language phenomenon in many fields, especially in translation studies. Based on the Adaptation Theory model proposed by Verschueren, the author puts forward her translation framework under the guidance of the Adaptation Theory. This can be shown in Figure 3-3.

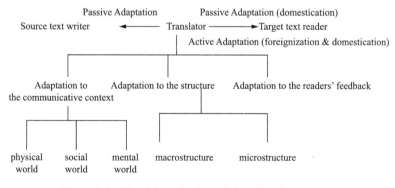

Figure 3-3   The Adaptation Translation Model

Translation as a three dimensional interaction among source text writer, translator and target text reader involves two layers of conversion. One takes place between the source text writer and the translator where translators make passive adaptations to the linguistic and contextual settings of the source text after comprehending the explicit and implicit meanings that the source text conveys. The other occurs between the translator and the target text reader where translators adapt both passively and actively to the target text. Passive adaptation denotes that translators should observe the target readers' cognitive, emotive, cultural and social norms without any changes. Domestication translation strategies are often employed in passive adaptation in that they focus on the reactions of the target readers. Active adaptation emphasizes translators' selection on word choice, structure, style and discourse to be fit for the target readers. During the translation process, translators face a lot of choices among which they can take the initiative to select the most appropriate and idiomatic version to the source text. Foreignization and domestication translation strategies are adopted in active adaptation in order to spread the home culture to the foreign people.

In the course of translation, translators as intermediators between source text and target text should adapt passively or actively to the source text's context, structure and readers' feedback. Context here mainly denotes the communicative context, that is, the physical world, mental world and social world. Adaptation to structure can be subdivided into macrostructure and microstructure. Macrostructure stands for the linguistic context, style and discourse while microstructure refers to sound, rhyme, word choice and syntax. Besides, readers' feedback to the translation text should be taken into account in that it will determine whether the versions will be accepted by most of the target readers. This model has great implications on translation of other text types, such as translation of advertisement, contract and literary works. In the following chapters, the author will employ this translation model to analyze translation of tourism texts.

3.2 Methodology

3.2.1 Research Questions

In order to investigate which dimension functions in tourism text translation, the author conducted a survey on translation of famous scenic spots in Shandong Province. This project lasted one month from December, 2006 to January, 2007. It aims to solve the following problems:

(1) How does adaptation function in tourism translation in terms of structures, physical world, mental world and social world?

(2) What are the Chinese students' translation problems in adaptation to tourism text?

3.2.2 Research Objects

As translation is an advanced competence which calls for a wide range of knowledge on English and Chinese as well as translation skills, the author randomly selects the research objects from students of doctor's, master's and bachelor's degrees. Most of them are born in Shandong Province in China. 130 questionnaires were collected from Tongji University, Shandong Normal University, Shandong Architecture and Engineering University and Shandong Mineral Institute, of which 108 were valid. The author then divided all the subjects into three types—30 non-English major postgraduates, 30 English-major postgraduates and 48 seniors. According to the conventional sampling standards (Chen Xiangming, 2000), each variable should contain no less than 20, the division of the 108 questionnaires was in fit with the conventional standard for further investigation.

3.2.3 Design of the Questionnaire

With the assumption that translation is a comprehensive process consisting of structural, physical, mental and social correlates, the author designed six samples of scenic spot translations among which five scenic spots were in Shandong Province and one was an advertisement about American city Huston. The fourth option in each multiple choice was presumed with the ideal translation strategy which took the target readers' structural, physical, mental and social worlds into account. Each sample represented a typical translation strategy, for instance, the second and sixth were the tests of structures; the first, the second and the fourth concerned the psychology; the third and fifth were the social impacts on the tourists. Meanwhile, in the third sample, physical deixis of time was investigated so as to know whether the readers had a cultural awareness on time (cf. Figure 3-1). Besides, some blurring choices like transliteration, word-for-word translation and literal translation easily committed by the students in tourism text translation were listed in the multiple choices. Each reader was required to tick out the right answer and then give a brief comment on the choices. Altogether, there were four multiple choices for every source text rendering. Each equally assigned a ratio of 25%. Any item which exceeded the percentage 25% would be regarded as high expectancy.

It should be noted by the author that a version may embody two adaptive translation strategies (such as Samples 1 and 2) which may influence the validity, but one adaptation strategy was dominantly tested in the translation process. Some scholars had different views on translation of Samples 1 and 2, because for the culture-loaded names of scenic spots, some wanted to publicize the Chinese culture to the outside world while others hoped to get the versions easily accepted by the foreign tourists. Bearing on mind that tourism text translation was a special genre to introduce more information and gain more acceptance by the foreign tourists, the author took a domestication-dominated translation strategy to account for the culture-loaded names of the scenic spots. See Table 3-1.

Table 3-1 Adaptability Manifested in the Survey

Adaptability / Number of the Questions	Adaptation to the Structure	Adaptation to the Physical World	Adaptation to the Mental World	Adaptation to the Social World
1			√	
2	√		√	
3		√		√
4			√	
5				√
6	√			

Note: " √ " signifies a version owns the characteristics of adaptability in the corresponding item. A version may have two or more translation strategies.

3.2.4   Reliability and Validity

The reasons to choose the students from the four universities are as follows: Firstly, they are credited with high-level education, which means they are equipped with a wider horizon and language competence than the counterparts. The students come from famous universities in Shandong and Shanghai and most of them are going to get the doctor's degree or master's degree, at least the bachelor's degree. Secondly, a large part of them are born and grown up in Shandong, which ensure them to be familiar with the five scenic spot samples of Shandong Province. Furthermore, some of them are fully aware of the stories and legends behind the scenic spots. Therefore, the awareness of the cultural background knowledge can be manifested on the students. Lastly, the questionnaires are handed out in a cozy environment without pressures. The content of the questionnaire does not concern with privacy or conflict with personal interest. By informing them that there is no definite answer to each version and they can tick out what they like without signatures, most of the students are pleased to finish this project.

The 108 questionnaires consisted of 30 non-English-major postgraduates, 30 English-major postgraduates and 48 seniors. It is reliable in accordance with the conventional sampling standards. (Chen Xiangming, 2000) Furthermore, to ensure the credibility of the questionnaire, the author interviewed all the participants to illustrate their translation process. Necessary changes had been made to render the versions more convincing.

3.3   Results

For the convenience of investigation, the author divided all the respondents into three types: English-major postgraduate, non-English-major postgraduate and seniors. In each type of samples, the statistics were equalized to testify the radio of acceptance. Any choice exceeding 25% would be received as high popularity. The option (D) in each multiple choice is regarded as the ideal adaptation translation strategy involving the structural, physical, mental and social correlates. Questionnaires for the English-major postgraduates are shown in Table 3-2.

Table 3-2   Results for the English-Major Postgraduates (N=30)

Multiple Choice Version Number	A		B		C		D		Reasons
	N	P	N	P	N	P	N	P	
1	13	43.3%	10	30%	3	10%	4	13.3%	simple, clear, cultural-specific
2	13	43.3%	3	10%	3	10%	11	36.7%	traditional, acceptable
3	0	0	7	23.3%	0	0	23	76.7%	cultural, proper, indirect, vivid
4	0	0	3	10%	7	23.3%	20	66.6%	attractive, aimed to show Chinese culture
5	0	0	0	0	13	43.3%	17	56.7%	including Chinese culture, dignity
6	3	10%	0	0	10	33.3%	17	56.7%	dynamic, imaginative

Note: N stands for number of the students, P stands for its percentage to the overall respondents.

It is not hard to find among the six sample translations that the third, the fourth, the fifth and the sixth show a high percentage of expectancy with the option (D), of which the third sample amounts to a percentage of 76.7%. As it was held by many students, those versions were "cultural, attractive and dynamic." People varied on the first and second sample translation. Hot debates were carried out on whether the place term should be transliterated or freely translated. 43.3% of the postgraduates chose transliteration in that they believed those versions promoted the ethnic Chinese culture to the outside world. For the second sample translation, "Bubbling Spring" was also well received for its vividness. How about the non-English-major postgraduates? Will they share a similar view with the English majors? This can be shown in Table 3-3.

Table 3-3   Results for the Non-English-Major Postgraduates (N=30)

Multiple Choice Version Number	A		B		C		D		Reasons
	N	P	N	P	N	P	N	P	
1	6	20%	18	30%	6	20%	0	0	
2	18	60%	12	40%	0	0	0	0	fit for the international rule
3	6	20%	11	36.7%	0	0	13	43.3%	
4	9	30%	3	10%	6	20%	12	40%	natural
5	6	20%	0	0	24	80%	0	0	
6	0	0	0	0	0	0	30	100%	heard from the text

The non-English-major postgraduates agreed on the third, the fourth and the sixth sample translations with the percentages of 43.3%, 40% and 100% respectively. Students totally appreciated the translation of Sample 6 because Qingdao as a Sailing City at the 2008 Olympic Games was often heard in TV, newspaper and radio, which also reflected that the postgraduate students were more concerned about the domestic affairs. By contrast, the first, the second and the fifth received a low frequency of popularity as a result of ethnics and lacking of corresponding social background knowledge. Comparing the results from the English-major postgraduates with non-English-major postgraduates, most of the expected answers from each sample were approved by the respondents. Will the same happen to the seniors? Please look at Table 3-4.

Table 3-4   Results for the Seniors (N=48)

Multiple Choice Version Number	A		B		C		D		Reasons
	N	P	N	P	N	P	N	P	
1	12	25%	17	35.4%	17	35.4%	2	4.1%	simple, clear, ethnic
2	16	33.3%	10	20.8%	11	22.9%	11	22.9%	ethnic

(to be continued)

Multiple Choice Version Number	A		B		C		D		Reasons
	N	P	N	P	N	P	N	P	
3	6	12.5%	11	22.9%	9	18.75%	22	45.8%	beautiful
4	2	4.2%	20	14.6%	19	39.6%	7	41.7%	
5	4	8.3%	8	16.7%	30	62.5%	6	12.5%	noble
6	19	39.6%	10	20.8%	9	18.8%	10	20.8%	

When translating the first and second samples characterized by shortness and brevity, 35.4% of the seniors agreed with transliteration in the first sample and 33.3% of the seniors had the same opinions on transliterating the second sample. Comparatively speaking, the cultural translation of the two scenic spots were relatively low with 4.1% and 22.9% respectively. The ones of higher expectancy went to Samples 3 and 4 while the results of Samples 5 and 6 were lower than the author's expectancy. This indicates that the respondents are equipped with a certain level of language competence, but are short of sufficient psychological knowledge and translation skills.

Taking all the three tables together, a large quantity of the results are in consistent with the author's expectancy as in Samples 3, 4 and 6. Sample 3 gets the highest mark, because most students believed that translation should be in fit with the target readers' physical and cultural background. Samples 4 and 6 are concerned with the linguistic conversion. Its relatively higher marks than the rest indicate students are skilled at linguistic competence. For the social correlates embedded in Sample 5, only a few non-English-major postgraduates and seniors get the right answer for lack of correspondent geographical knowledge.

There is incongruence with the author's expectancy in Samples 1 and 2. People varied their opinions on whether those versions should be transliterated or freely translated. For Sample 1, 33.3% of the English-major postgraduates and 60% of the non-English-major postgraduates voted for transliteration in that it helped to spread Chinese culture to the Western countries. By contrast, the adaptive translation to the foreigner's cultural context was only accepted by the advanced-level language learners. It should be noted that students' cultural translation skills should be strengthened.

To sum up, the questionnaire testifies the author's presumption of tourism text translation as a multi-dimensional conversion involving the co-functioning of structural, physical, psychological and social correlates, which provides the feasibility of the Adaptation Theory in tourism text translation. Students need not only develop the linguistic competence, but also foster the cultural and social awareness during translation. In the following sections, the author will analyze the tourism texts translation from the above angles under the framework of Adaptation Theory.

Chapter 4
Adaptation to the Structure in Tourism Text Translation

Researches on adaptation to the structure in tourism text translation are conducted from the macro and micro angles. Microstructure analyzes the elements in the sentential level where phonetic, lexical, syntactic and stylistic ingredients are taking effects. What matters greatly in the translation of microstructure are the grammatical confinements. When the variances between original and target texts take place, changes must be made to adapt to the grammatical rules of the target language. Macrostructure focuses attention above the sentence. The embedded sequential orders like the chronological, spatial and logical orders will guarantee which sentence in the paragraph goes first. Translators are permitted to alter the orders to meet with the target readers' reading habits. Especially in Chinese to English translation, some English idiomatic devices like the discourse markers, participles and prepositional phrases are added to make the text more coherent and logical. In the whole process of adaptation to the structure in tourism text translation, translators first adapt passively to the grammatical limitation by the target languages. Meanwhile, to achieve preciseness and vividness in the target text, active adaptations like the choices on words, syntax and rhymes are made by the translators to coincide with the style of the source text. It should be noted that active adaptation to the target text structure manifests the translator's manipulation on words. Nida once said, "In order to translate the meaning, form must be changed." Another Chinese essayist and translator Si Guo in his *New Researches in Translation* spoke out the essence of translation, "Translation is not translating literally, but a rewrite of the source text." Active adaptation translation occurs more to the cultural elements where the translators aim to spread the home culture to the foreign tourists.

4.1 Lexical Level

Lexical adaptation concentrates on the correctness and appropriateness of word choices in the sentence. Chinese belongs to the Sino-Tibetan language system while English can be included in the Indo-European language families, which leads to the strikingly differences in linguistics. In terms of lexis, English is abundant in nouns and prepositions whereas Chinese is rich in verbs; there are articles as "a, an, the" in English but Chinese language does not distinguish their differences; when counting things, Chinese adds quantifiers between numerals and nouns. For instance, in the phrases " 五棵树 " (meaning five trees) and " 六朵花 " (meaning six flowers), " 棵 " and " 朵 " are quantifiers to modify the nouns "trees" and "flowers" respectively, but the English equivalences seldom use such quantifiers. As regards for tourism text— a branch of literature variety, Chinese prefer to express their love to the natural scenery and historical sites by means of four-character phrases, allusions and poems. On the contrary, English is featured by brevity as is illustrated by the limited number of adjectives to describe the scenic spots. Therefore, translators need to adapt to the target texts to be in compliance with the linguistic confinements. Adaptation to the lexical differences in tourism text translation is manifested in the word choice and word collocation. The importance of word choice is revealed by Jonathan Swift in his famous saying, "Proper words in proper places make the true definition of a style." We may illustrate this point by the following example.

Example 4-1   ST: 帆船之都
          TT: the Sailing City

The source text is a noun phrase with a noun "帆船" (sail) functioning as an adjective to modify the other noun "都" (the city). In rendering the source text, the translator changed the adjectival noun into the present participle "sailing," which symbolized the dynamics and vitality of the city. The dynamic present participle displayed to the foreign tourists that Qingdao was a growing city characterized by vibrancy. Besides, when the 2008 Olympic Game took place, the word "sailing" reminded the foreign tourists of the city as a host to hold a sailing competition. No wonder millions of foreign tourists would long to pay a visit to this beautiful coastal city. In the questionnaire the author conducted, 100% of the non-English-major postgraduates agreed with the version. Translators' active adaptation in words can also be shown in the following example.

Example 4-2　ST: The mildness of its climate with slight temperature, variations and infrequent rainfall, combined with a high average level of sunshine and brilliant skies all make it ideal for tourism whether by winter or by summer.

TT: 本地区气温稳定，雨水稀少，阳光充裕，天空晴朗，是冬夏皆宜的旅游胜地。

(Lu Min, 2005)

The ideal tourism resort boasts moderate temperature, rainfall, sunshine and sky. In the source text, the writer employed four adjectives "slight, infrequent, high, brilliant" to modify the mildness of climate. With the emphasis on the list of scenes, the source text seemed short and brief. However, in the organization of text, Chinese tourism texts love to employ symmetrical structures like antithesis and parallelism to express their love to nature, emphasizing the oneness of human and nature. Therefore, the above Chinese versions employed five four-character phrases to express appreciation to the natural beauty with an antithesis structure. Thus, through the use of antithesis, the translator in the above example adapted to Chinese writing habits and the aesthetics of the target text was increased accordingly.

Word choice can also be demonstrated in the appropriateness of words. Different registers call for different word choices. Formal words are often used in law and diplomatic documents. Latin words frequently appear in the medicine books, and long complex scholarly words pervade in the academic books. In daily conversation, informal slang words are often encountered. As for literary language, word choice is much more important since it concerns about the beauty and style of the text. Translation of tourism text must be carried out with great care to correspond to the style of the original text. For instance,

Example 4-3 ST: The cheapest way to reach Britain from continental Europe is to swim across the English channels; this requires extra-ordinary stamina and has been tackled by a handful of budget travelers.
TT: 从欧洲大陆来大不列颠旅行,最省钱的方式当数泅渡;但这需要超人的耐力,迄今仅有几个"老抠"办到过。

(Wang Zhikui, 2002)

The source text is a humorous tourism text. The English Channel runs across Britain and continental Europe with a width of 250 kilometers from the southwest. It is impossible for travelers to swim across the English Channel, but this way of transport was used by a few "budget" travelers in that it was the cheapest way. Moreover, the humor lies in the word "budget." Budget is a formal financial term, which originally means an estimate of expected income and expenses. It seems ridiculous to put a formal technical term in a mix of ordinary words, but that is where humor lies. The translator adapted to the humorous style of the source text with a Chinese equivalence "老抠" (a Chinese slang phrase to refer to a mean person like Shylock in English). Such a phrase corresponds to the style of the source, adding much vividness and humor to the version.

Word collocation signifies the habitual or expected co-occurrence regulations of words in the sentence. Any lexical word will have its corresponding recurring collocate in the contexts. For instance, in English, adjectives are often put in front of nouns and adverbs usually follow the verbs. Translators should observe the collocation limitations in the scope of the target text grammar.

Example 4-4 ST: Visitors will enjoy such events as musical performances, fine art shows, craft fairs, the New England Antique Boat Museum, fireworks and many other activities.

TT: 游客在这儿可以<u>出席</u>音乐会，<u>欣赏</u>美术展览和工艺品展览，<u>参观</u>新英格兰古代船舶博物馆，晚上还可<u>观看</u>焰火 —— 活动项目丰富多彩，令你应接不暇。

(Lu Min, 2005)

The source text is a simple sentence with one verb "enjoy" as the predicate and six nouns as the objects of the verb. This may reflect the fact that English people anticipate the touring activities to be participated. Yet in Chinese it seemed too general and monotonous for one verb to be accompanied by six nouns. In translating the verb "enjoy," the translator actively employed four consecutive verbs to collocate with the corresponding nouns, promoted the language vividness and emphasized the tourists' participation in the tour. Furthermore, the four verb phrases formed a parallelism structure to increase the beauty of the text.

4.2 Syntactic Level

An English compound sentence can be divided into a main clause with several subordinate sentences. The complex structure of the English sentence is like a tree full of branches, hence gets the name by the grammarian the branching structure. A Chinese sentence progresses in line with the spatial, chronological and logical orders. Clauses are separated by commas to represent the meaning progression from the speakers' point of view. Like a flowing river, the Chinese sentence is named as the watering structure. Translators should adapt to the syntactic variances between the two languages.

Example 4-5   ST: 天贶殿是岱庙的主殿，为古代帝王祭祀泰山神的地方，建于1009 年。

TT: Built in 1009 during the Song dynasty, the Tiankuang Hall, the chief building of the Dai Temple, was the place where the emperors of the ancient times offered sacrifices to the God of Mount Tai.

(Zhou Changjun & Zhang Zhongshui, 2004)

The source text is an tourism instruction on Tiankuang Hall in Dai Temple at the foot of Mount Tai in Shandong Province, China. Information on the hall was provided through three separated short sentences accounting for what, why and when the hall was built, which progressed in line with the logical meanings. However, in the English version the main clause was modified by a past participle, an apposition and an adverbial clause of place. With one embedded in another, the whole sentence looked more complex than the Chinese text.

Syntactic variances between Chinese and English in the sentential level in tourism text can be manifested in four aspects: long sentences and short sentences, conversion of the sentence order, hypotaxis and parataxis, passive voice and active voice.

4.2.1   Long Sentences and Short Sentences

The English language is abundant in long sentences while the Chinese language is rich in short sentences. Long sentences contain detailed complex structures and multiple layers of meaning. They make the statements formal and logical with little misunderstandings. Ju Yumei (1999) pointed out that in literary writing, long sentences "describe quick successive actions or feelings, simultaneous or continuous action, or indicate a close cause and effect relationship." Short sentences always appear in daily conversation, advertisement and slogans. Being short and brief, the short sentences increase the vividness and forcefulness of the text. Comparing the English text with the Chinese text in tourism texts, we get the conclusion that English tourism texts are abundant in long sentences while the Chinese ones are rich in short sentences. Translation of long sentences should be based on the correct analysis of the syntax in the source text. Grasp the central idea and layers of subordinate meanings, analyze the chronological, spatial and logical orders that the source text connotes, and then translate the text according to the requirements of the target language. Techniques like division, integration and reversal of orders may be needed to enhance the efficiency of translation.

Example 4-6   ST: Outside the industrial areas the countryside is remarkable for

the wonderful variety of shades of green in the fields and trees—
a delicacy and subtlety of color not to be found in other places, and
reflecting the lack of extremes in the climate.

TT: 工业区外的乡村是田野与树木的天地,郁郁葱葱,青绿相间,
美不胜收;色彩之细微与清淡,世上独有,由此可见这儿的气候温
和宜人。

(Lu Min, 2005)

The source is a long sentence depicting the greenness of the countryside
outside the industrial areas. The first part is a simple sentence followed by a dash
expounding on the specialty of the color "green." A literal rendering of the source
sounds non-idiomatic and unnatural. So the translator technically divided it into
seven short sentences among which three paralleled four-character phrases increased
the beauty and vigor of the text. In addition, the commenting word "remarkable"
at the beginning of the source text was placed at the end of the Chinese version.
Habitually, Chinese prefer to put the most important information till the end while
English people put forward the topic sentence at the beginning. In accordance with
Chinese habits, the translator actively put the commenting words to the end to render
the Chinese version idiomatic.

Conversion of long sentences and short sentences in tourism text translation
will also be influenced by other factors like the chronological, spatial, logical
orders and the writer's point of view. Translators should take the overall factors into
account and adapt flexibly to the source. Limited by the space, the author will not
give a detailed account on it.

4.2.2 Conversion of the Sentence Order

English-speaking people are frank and always put forward the topic sentence
once the text begins. On the contrary, Chinese people are conservative to reserve the
focal points until the end. Translators must pay attention to the obvious variances in
the organization.

Example 4-7 ST: 灵岩寺坐落在群山怀抱之中,这里峰峦奇秀,松柏葱郁,谷深景幽,泉石秀丽,风光旖旎,四季宜人。

TT: Surrounded on all the sides by mountains, the Lingyan Temple presents charming and pleasant scenery of spectacular peaks and ridges, abundant verdant pines and cypresses, deep valleys and secluded landscape as well as beautiful springs and rocks.

(Zhou Changjun & Zhang Zhongshui, 2004)

The Chinese source text provides a vivid description of the Lingyan Temple with six four-character words functioning as antithesis and parallelism to reinforce the pleasant scenery. However, the comment of the sentence "四季宜人," that is, the wonderful scenery of the temple in the four seasons, was not proposed until the end of the sentence. Literal translation will keep the English readers wonder the topic for a long time and lose patience. Thus the translator spoke out directly the theme before listing the scenic spots. The conversion of sentence order coincided with the English organization of texts.

4.2.3 Hypotaxis and Parataxis

Another obvious difference in English and Chinese is hypotaxis and parataxis. The English language is linked by the explicit grammatical means, including discourse markers, conjunctions and so on. Joined by them, every part in English sentences could be embedded to modify each other in chain; hence it is featured by hypotaxis (means to be linked by forms). The clauses in a Chinese sentence are ordered through the logical meanings without any auxiliary means, so a Chinese sentence is featured by parataxis (means to be linked by meaning). Conversion of hypotaxis and parataxis is common in the tourism translation.

Example 4-8 ST: If tickets are not available, we are not going out for picnic.

TT: 没票,我们就不去野餐了。

The source text is an adverbial clause of condition with the word "if" serving as the connectives. The Chinese version omitted the conditional linking words and substituted it with two clauses joined by the embedded logical meanings. This arrangement rendered the text brief and idiomatic.

Example 4-9   ST: 其特点是用鲜活材料制成,保持原汁原味,美味可口。

TT: With fresh vegetables and live fowl or fish as ingredients, one can savor the dishes for their natural flavor.

(Lu Min, 2005)

In the source text, the first clause constitutes a cause-and-effect relationship with the second clause because it signifies the reason why one can savor the dish's natural flavor. When translating the source text, the translator actively added a prepositional "with" phrase to clarify the reason. Readers will easily sense the logical relationship with the help of the adding preposition.

4.2.4 Passive Voice and Active Voice

Passive voice is widely used in English tourism text when there is no need for the agent, or the writer is reluctant to mention the agent. Chinese text also has passive voice which usually has derogatory meanings, and it has a lower frequency than the active voice. Thus conversions of passive voice and active voice are needed in the translation of Chinese and English texts.

Example 4-19   ST: 同时,山东省还围绕生态省建设,进一步加大植树造林力度。目前,全省人工造林面积 141.1 千公顷。共建成 12 个国家生态示范区,创建了 20 个生态建设示范县,建成各类自然保护区 74 处。全省森林覆盖率达到 24%。

TT: Centering on building up an ecological province, Shandong is making concerted efforts to afforest the land by planting trees. At present, throughout the province, the area of man-planted forest has hit 141,100 hectares. Twelve national demonstration areas of ecology have been constructed, 20 demonstration "ecological countries" have been set up, and 74 natural reserves have been established, so the percentage of forest cover in Shandong has hit 24%.

(Information Office of Shandong Provincial People's Government, 2006)

The above passage is extracted from a publicity pamphlet of Shandong Province. In the publicity register, Chinese texts often stress the achievements of the governments which act as the subject explicitly or implicitly. However, in the English publicity texts, the functions of the government are seldom mentioned. Therefore, three passive voices are adopted in the target text as underlined in the examples.

4.2.5 Phonetic Devices

As an expressive and vocative text, the tourism text specializes in the aesthetics of languages so as to arouse tourists' interest. One of the effective devices is the use of sounds. Onomatopoeia, alliteration, assonance, consonance and pun in the tourism text present a vivid picture of the scenic spots.

Onomatopoeia is the imitation of sounds for effect. It adds the vividness and vitality to the text. During translation, we may adopt the equivalent onomatopoetic words if they exist in the corresponding target text or ignore them depending on the actual context. In the following example, the translator used the onomatopoetic "gurgling" to depict the sound of the flowing water, endowing the text with much vitality.

Example 4-11   ST: 九溪十八涧以 " 叮叮咚咚水，弯弯曲曲路 " 而著称。

TT: The place called Nine Creeks and Eighteen Gullies is well known for its twisting paths and gurgling streams.

(Gu Shusen, 2001)

Alliteration is the repetition of the first consonant in two or more words. It is often found in idioms, proverbs and tongue twisters. In tourism text, it often takes place in tourist advertisement. The following is an advertisement translation on the American fourth biggest city Huston cited from *National Geography*.

Example 4-12　ST: Starlight on Skyline, Galaxy of Glamour.

　　　　　　　TT1: 高楼摩天, 星光灿烂; 火树银花, 瑰丽绝伦。

(Bao Huinan & Bao Ang, 2004)

　　　　　　　TT2: 高楼摩天, 星光灿烂; 火树银花, 美轮美奂。

(Translated by the author)

The source text strikes the readers as two repetitions of consonants "s" and "g," reinforcing the content to the hearers. Furthermore, the use of sibilant "s" leaves a soft and gentle impression on the readers, who will feel comfortable on hearing the advertisement. However, it will be a tough job to translate the source with the same devices. In the first Chinese version, the translator cleverly changed alliteration into consonance (repetition on the final consonant) rhyming on the words "天" and "烂" with a feet on /an/. Besides, four four-character phrases were used as antithesis to increase the elegance of the text. Even though they were not with the same devices, the effects of the English source text did not decrease as a result of the translator's clever adaptation to the Chinese text. But could we change the last Chinese phrase into "美轮美奂" in that it formed a rhymed "aaba" with the above lines? Among the six questions the author surveyed in the questionnaire, this version got the highest marks. 66.6% of the English-major postgraduates, 40% of the non-English-major postgraduates and 41.7% of the seniors voted for this version.

Assonance and consonance are predominant in poetic languages to produce an effect of euphony. Assonance is a repetition of vowel sounds in the stressed syllables of a series of words while consonance repeats the last consonant syllable. To make it clear, the author will illustrate it by the following example.

Example 4-13　ST: 重重叠叠山, 曲曲环环路, 叮叮咚咚泉, 上上下下树。

　　　　　　　TT: The hills—range after range,

　　　　　　　The trails—winding and climbing;

　　　　　　　The creeks—murmuring and gurgling;

　　　　　　　The trees—high and lowly.

(Chen Gang, 2004)

The Chinese text employed repetitious words to modify the hills, roads, creams and trees, highlighting the symmetrical beauty of Chinese languages. To achieve the same effects, the translator creatively produced the consonance of "l" in "hills" and "trails" and of "ing" in "winding and climbing," which was assonance of the vowel /aɪ/ as well. Meanwhile, assonance is also achieved by the use of /i:/ in the pairs "creeks and trees." Other devices like onomatopoeia "murmuring and gurgling" and repetition "range" were used in the English version to increase the euphony. Thus reading the English version is like reading a poem, enhancing the visual and aural pleasures to the readers. Sometimes a nonce-word is created to reach special effects.

Example 4-14   ST: 有什么能比钓鱼更有味？

TT: What could be <u>delisher</u> than fisher?

(Wu Yun, 2004)

The nonce-word "delisher," imitating the word "delicious," implies the fish would be yummy. At the same time, consonance of /ə/ in "delisher" and "fisher" fills the English version with euphony. This translation presents to us the translator's talented manipulation over words.

4.3 Stylistic Level

People travel to the other places not only for the knowledge, but also for fun and relaxation. A series of rhetorical devices enhance the readers' aesthetic values. The tourism text, as a vocative text to express emotions, is always written elegantly by means of simile, metaphor, poetry, repetition, parallelism and other devices. Such devices amount to the literariness of the text. Translators should work out the ways to retain the style of the source text.

4.3.1 Simile and Metaphor

Simile is the comparison of two different things sharing at least one quality in common with the word "like" or "as." There are similes both in English and Chinese, thus on most occasions, a literal translation can definitely show the similarities between the texts.

Example 4-15　ST: 大明湖似一颗璀璨的明珠，镶嵌在泉城之中；黄河如带，蜿蜒由西向东。

TT: The Daming Lake, just like a bright pearl, is inlaid in the Spring City. The Yellow River winds its way from west to east like a narrow ribbon.

(Zhou Changjun & Zhang Zhongshui, 2004)

Contrary to simile, metaphor studies the comparison of two different things sharing at least one quality in common without the word "like" or "as." Metaphor has a high frequency in the practical translation text, especially in tourism text. A literal translation is needed in translation of metaphor in tourism text, but sometimes free translation is employed as a result of cultural losses.

Example 4-16　ST: 芙蓉街位于济南中心地区，北临大明湖，南靠繁华的商业街泉城路，周围是古城区护城河。

TT: The Furong Street Historic Section is situated in the heart of Jinan encircled by the ancient city moat, with the Daming Lake to the north and Quancheng Road (a vibrant and active commercial street) to the south, covering an area of 47 hectares.

(Zhou Changjun & Zhang Zhongshui, 2004)

The Furong Street plays a vital role in Jinan's economic and cultural life the same way as the heart does to the human body. The translator highlighted the importance of the city by comparing it to the heart. The utility of the city thus was vividly presented to the readers. Sometimes translators have to make changes to adapt to the culture of the destination.

Example 4-17　ST: 欲把西湖比西子，淡妆浓抹总相宜。

TT1: West Lake may be compared to Beauty Xi Zi at her best,

It becomes her to be richly adorned or plainly dressed.

TT2: West Lake may be compared to Beauty Cleopatra at her best,
It becomes her to be richly adorned or plainly dressed.

(Chen Gang, 2004)

Xi Zi is ranked as one of the four great beauties in ancient China, who helped the King Gou Jian of Yue Kingdom regain the lost land. In the source text, West Lake was compared to the beauty Xi Zi for its wonderful scenery. Lacking of shared cultural background information, a literal translation would puzzle the tourists. Chinese translator Chen Gang practiced to foreground the Beauty Xi Zi by comparing her to the Egyptian Queen Cleopatra. Besides in the English version, he added "at her best" to supplement the cultural loss. Such an active adaptation would receive applause and high praise from the tourists each time he translated the poem. Adaptation in metaphor translation can also be shown in the following:

Example 4-18   ST: As one of the Four Tigers in Asia, Hong Kong is also known as the Oriental Pearl and the Shopping Paradise.
TT: 作为亚洲四小龙之一的香港，同样被誉为"东方之珠"和"购物天堂"。

(Wang Zhikui, 2002)

Tiger in the English context is regarded as the king of jungles with supreme power. Hong Kong in the source text was compared to the tiger to symbolize its paramount economic situation. In China, the responsibility to rule over the animals in the forest is taken on by "龙" (Chinese Dragon God). Therefore, the translator replaced tigers with Chinese Dragon God to retain the pragmatic effects. The same translation strategy can be applied to the translation of "五龙潭." Can we apply the principle by translating the phrase as "Five Tiger Pool?" However, according to the survey, this adaptation has lower acceptability, only 13.3% of the English-major postgraduates acknowledged the version. Therefore, infusing the cultural knowledge to the students during teaching is necessary to improve the translation skills of the future students.

4.3.2　Poetry

Poems are widely used in Chinese tourism text to show the writer's love to the natural scenery. Readers may meet with dozes of poems, allusions, quotations and antithesis in the Chinese tourism text. But that is not the case in the English text. As Connor (2001) put it, "These poems, sayings, and allusions are used to ornament and enliven discourse in Chinese writing, but to the Western reader they are distractions and make the text lack argumentative coherence." The English tourism texts plainly list the scenic spots, describe the adventurous experience from the tour, or comment on the amusement or other comforting facilities they may get during the tour. Thus, translators have to reduce or omit the superfluous poems if they are not coherent with the themes of the text.

Example 4-19　ST: "烟水苍茫月色迷,渔舟晚泊栈桥西。乘凉每至黄昏后,人依栏杆水拍堤。"这是古人赞美青岛海滨的诗句。青岛是一座风光秀丽的海滨城市,夏无酷暑,冬无严寒。西起胶州湾入海处的团岛,东至崂山风景区的下清宫,绵延 80 多华里的海滨组成了一幅绚丽多姿的长轴画卷。

TT: Qingdao is a charming coastal city, whose beauty often appears in poetry. It is not hot in summer or cold in winter. Its 40 km-long scenic line begins from Tuandao at the west and to Xiaqing Temple of Laoshan Mountain at the east end.

(Information Office of Qingdao Municipal People's Government, 2002)

The source text gives us a brief introduction on Qingdao's climate and location. Poems enhance the beauty of language, but are redundant in the English version for their low frequency in the English tourism text. So the translator omitted the poems by starting the paragraph with a topic sentence—"Qingdao is a charming coastal city," which generalized the topic of the paragraph.

4.3.3　Parallelism

Parallelism is the repetition of the same structural patterns in three or more sentences. It foregrounds the central ideas by the frequent use of a pattern and balances the sentences with more clarity and coherence. Parallelism is one of the most commonly used rhetorical devices in tourism text in that it promotes the vigor of the text. Both English and Chinese have parallelism in the tourism text. In C-E or E-C translation, literal or free translation would be adopted depending on the context.

Example 4-20   ST: (红叶谷)景区内绿荫浓郁,群山苍翠,碧波剪影。春天山花烂漫,夏天凉爽宜人。深秋红叶流丹,冬天红梅傲雪。

TT: The site is shaded by green trees, surrounded by mountains and mirrored in clear waters. In spring, bright-colored flowers in full bloom can be found here and there on the mountains. In summer, it enjoys a pleasant weather with cool breezes. In autumn, it is covered with red leaves. In winter, plum waves proudly in snow.

(Zhou Changjun & Zhang Zhongshui, 2004)

The charming scenery of the Red Leaves Valley in the four seasons of a year was displayed to the readers by parallelism in the source text. Four four-character phrases depicting the valleys in the four seasons increased the literariness and elegance of the text. But that strategy is not fit for the English tourism texts because English is characterized by brevity. English people wonder more about the information of destination, itinerary or accommodation during the traveling. Thus a literal and plain translation is provided. Occasionally, even though there is no parallelism in the English source text, translators could add one to correspond to the writing habits of the Chinese tourism text.

Example 4-21   ST: Here in New Hampshire there are many opportunities to find a peaceful spot hidden among the lush forests of all tall evergreens and hard-woods or next to a rambling brook or pictorial lake.

TT: 新罕布什尔州森林茂密,绿树常青,泉水蜿蜒而流,湖边风景如画,到处都是幽然寂静的好去处。

(Lu Min, 2005)

New Hampshire, located in America, boasts forests, hard-woods, brooks and lakes. In the source, the writer simply listed the scenic spots with adjectives before them, signifying the brevity of the English text. However, a word-for-word translation in Chinese tourism text will be too plain and monotonous. The translator instead selected four s-v phrases to construct a parallelism. Like folding a picture before the readers, the Chinese text will be appreciated by more Chinese tourists.

4.3.4 Repetition

Repetition in literary texts serves for emphasis or balance of structures. It occurs either at the lexical level or in syntactic structures. There is repetition both in English and Chinese texts, but the Chinese texts are more frequent with repetition.

Example 4-22   ST: (即使住上五星级的饭店)金窝银窝，不如自家的草窝。

TT: Gold <u>home</u> or silver <u>home</u>, the sweetest is one's own <u>home</u>.

(Chen Gang, 2004)

When reading the Chinese source text, the readers can't help thinking of one famous saying in English, "East or west, home is the best." The translator adapted to the source text with the similar theme of homesickness. The word "home" was repeated three times for emphasis. The literariness and vividness in the English version will surely impress the readers greatly.

Repetition in the Chinese text takes place much more frequently than the English counterpart. As a rhetorical device for emphasis, repetition is widely adopted by Chinese writers to keep the balance of sentences even though it is redundant to the central ideas. Translators may reduce or omit the repetition to suit with the style of the English text.

Example 4-23   ST: 千佛山是泰山的余脉，东西绵亘，翠峰连绵，重峦叠嶂，松柏蓊郁，犹如济南的一道天然屏障。

TT: Just like a natural screen for protecting Jinan, the Thousand-Buddha Hill stretches from west to east with range upon range of mountains with verdant pine trees and cypresses.

(Zhou Changjun & Zhang Zhongshui, 2004)

Four four-character phrases in the source text with antithesis and parallelism improve the vibrancy and elegance of the text. Among the four four-character phrases, the second and the third meant one and the same thing—the mountains. In the translation, the translator incorporated them into one phrase "range upon range of mountains." Such adaptation made the text brief and clear, demonstrating the translator's talented translation skills.

4.3.5　Other Devices

There are other devices in the tourism text, such as personification, pun, and antithesis. Nord (2000) once pointed out, "The appellative function may be achieved indirectly through linguistic or stylistic devices that point to a referential or expressive function, such as superlatives, adjectives or nouns expressing positive values. The appellative function may even operate in poetic language appealing to the readers' aesthetic sensitivity. " On most occasions, the devices are literally translated if there are equivalences in the counterparts. But from time to time, free translation is employed for special purposes.

Example 4-24　ST: 趵突泉

　　　　　　　TT1: the Baotu Spring

　　　　　　　TT2: the Bubbling Spring

(Translated by the author)

The name of the spring " 趵突泉 " is a homonym of " 爆流泉 " which vividly describes the eruptive bubbling spring water. The first version literally translated it into Chinese Pinyin to foreground the Chinese characteristics. In the second version, the experimenting "bubbling" picked by the author was a pun in that it not only imitated the bubbling state of the flowing spring, but also mimicked the gurgling sounds of " 趵 " (Bao). 36.7% of the English major postgraduates voted for the second version.

4.4　Discourse Level

So far we've analyzed the translator's active and passive adaptation in tourism text translation in the sentential levels. Translators' adaptability can also be demonstrated in the translation of a discourse. In the organization of the discourse, Chinese usually leave the focal points till the end while the English put them forward as the topic sentence at the beginning of a paragraph. Translators thus should actively change the sentence orders to suit with the writing habits. Other influential factors like the cohesion and sequencing orders should be also taken into account. Generally speaking, adaptation in the discourse translation is manifested in changing the sentence orders or the use of linking verbs.

Example 4-25　ST: 市属三市二县内，北有超山，西有天目山。溯钱塘江而上，有富阳鹤山、桐庐瑶林仙境、桐君山、严子峻钓台、建德灵栖三洞、新安江千岛湖等名胜，形成一个以西湖为中心的广阔旅游区。

TT: The beauty spots in the vicinity of Hangzhou form a vast area for tourists with West Lake at its center. To the north of Hangzhou stands Chaoshan Hill, and to the east Mount Tianmu. Going up the Qiantang River, one finds oneself at Stork Hill near the Terrace where Yan Ziling, a hermit of the Eastern Han dynasty (25-220), loved to go fishing by the Funchun River in Fuyang City. Nearby are the Yaolin Wonderland in Tonglu Country, Tongjun Hill and the three Lingqi Caves in Jiande City, and finally the Thousand-Islet Lake at the source of Xin'anjiang River.

(Gu Shusen, 2001)

There are two sentences in the Chinese paragraph. Centering on a vast area for tourists with West Lake at the center, the Chinese writer first explained the geographical locations of Hangzhou City before arriving at the theme. The translator in the English version instead wrote out the theme first and then gave an explanation on it, which seemed more idiomatic for the English text. Translators' adaptability in the passage level can also be displayed in the use of linking verbs.

Example 4-26　ST: 青岛坐落在山东半岛南部, 依山临海, 天资秀美, 气候凉爽, 人称"东方瑞士"。白天, 青岛宛如镶嵌在黄海边的绿宝石, 夜里则像一只在大海中摆动的摇篮。难怪许多人乐意来这里疗养。

TT: Qingdao, known as the "the Switzerland of the Orient," is situated on the southern tip of Shandong Peninsula. Wedged between hills and waters, the city is endowed with beautiful scenery and a delightful climate. By day, she looks like an emerald inlaid in the coastline of the Yellow Sea and, at night, a cradle rocking upon the sea waves. No wonder so many people would like to seek rest and relaxation here.

(Lu Naisheng & Jin Yingying, 2000)

There are two sentences in the source text, the first of which is made up of five clauses. The first sentence is a cause-and-effect sentence because it states the reason of being called "the Switzerland of the Orient." So the translator employed the discourse marker "as" to clarify the relationship. Likewise, the second clause in the first sentence showed the reason for the third and fourth clauses in the same sentence. The translator correspondingly took the past participle "wedged" to denote the reason. Those linking words rendered the English version clear and coherent. If a passage is not written logically, the translator has the right to adjust the text to the central idea.

Example 4-27　ST: Although the state (Hawaii) is located in the tropical zone, its climate is comfortable because of the ocean currents that pass its shores and winds that blow across the land from the northeast. The temperature usually remains close to the annual average of 24 degrees centigrade.

TT: 夏威夷地处热带, 气候却温和宜人, 年均温度在 24 摄氏度左右。岛上时时刮过的东北风, 伴随着太平洋吹来的阵阵海风, 让人倍感舒适。

(Jia Wenbo,2004)

The last sentence in the source text told us how enjoyable Hawaii's climate was. It was an extension of the "comfortable climate" in the main clause of the first sentence. When translating the source, the translator merged the mild climate in the first sentence with 24 degrees centigrade as a complete sentence, which strengthened the unity of the text.

In accordance with the structural requirements for the target text, adaptation has to be made to render the version more coherent. No matter in the macro or micro levels, passive and active adaptive strategies in the translation flexibly coincide with the grammar rules of the target text as well as improving the vividness and literariness of the tourism text. Surely, adaptive translation will be more easily accepted by the foreign tourists than the literal translation for its cultural adaptation.

Chapter 5
Adaptation to the Physical World in Tourism Text Translation

Context is the co-occurrence of words or phrases in a particular setting that helps to infer the special meanings. In 1923, Malinowski coined the term "context of situation," holding that "Exactly as in the reality of spoken or written languages, a word without linguistic context is a mere figment and stands for nothing by itself, so in the reality of a spoken linguistic tongue, the utterance has no meaning except in the context of situation." Firth, following Malinowski, argued that language should be studied at all levels in its context of situation and with an emphasis on meaning. He further developed context of situation as containing the cultural setting of speech and the personal history of the participants rather than as simply the context of human activity going on at that moment. Sperber & Wilson (2001) considered context as assumptions present in the hearer's mind at the start of an utterance. Hearers inferred speaker's intention through an ostensive-inferential model. In 2000, Verschueren, in his *Understanding Pragmatics*, divided context into linguistic context and communicative context. Linguistic context, featured by cohesion, intertextuality and sequencing, was not what we focused on because we categorized it into the macrostructure world. Communicative context, according to Verschueren, consisted of physical world, mental world and social world. Those aspects more or less influenced the generation of the structure in the tourism text. Therefore, translation on communicative context should conform to the physical, social and psychological restrictions in the destination country. This will be discussed one by one in detail in the following sections.

According to Verschueren, physical world mainly referred to the temporal reference and spatial reference in the text. Besides, the harmonious relationship between utterer and interpreter and indispensable material conditions of speech contributed to the successful ongoing communication. In terms of tourism text translation, adaptations to the physical world are translator's proper handling of deixis, that is, the deixis of time, place and person.

5.1　Deixis of Time

Verschueren (2000) defined the deixis of time as the indicators of time, which were manifested through the event time, time of utterance and reference time. China has a splendid history of over 5,000 years, undergoing the replacement of several dynasties. There are dozens of stories and legends concerning the history of China in the Chinese tourism text, which may be unfamiliar to the foreign tourists. Translators should position the proper time in the source text by adding or omitting the temporal deixis to familiarize it with the foreign tourists, and sometimes a total adaptation is needed to fit with the tourists' cognitive environment.

Example 5-1　ST: 千佛山历史悠久，古称历山。据《水经注》记载，"相传上古时舜帝耕田于此"，故又称舜耕山。东晋时，佛教传入济南，千佛山成为人们祭祀舜帝的地方。隋开皇年间，佛教徒在山上依山凿窟，雕刻佛像千尊之多，并建千佛寺（即现在的兴国禅寺），因此，人们又称为千佛山。

TT: Known as the Lishan Hill in ancient times, the Thousand-Buddha Hill has a long history. According to *The River Annotation*, legend has it that Emperor Shun (a famous primitive king who successfully controlled the floods to save the people) in the primitive period once toiled at the foot of the hill, hence the hill got another name the Shun

Toiling Hill. In the Eastern Jin dynasty (317-420), with the advent of Buddhism into Jinan, the hill came to be the place where people offered sacrifices to Emperor Shun. During the reign of the Sui dynasty (581-618), Buddhist followers cut grottos on the cliffs and carved thousands of statues of Buddha in them.

(Extracted from Baidu Wenku)

The tourism text accounts for the origin of the name Thousand-Buddha Hill. Three great events involved in naming of the hill were developed through a chronological order among which were the primitive period, the Eastern Jin dynasty and the Sui dynasty. The foreign tourists might be unfamiliar with the changes of Chinese dynasties. The translator added the timing of the two periods by bracket, through which foreign tourists would have a clear view on the time of the events. Adding the specific time period for Chinese dynasties promotes foreigners' understanding on the Chinese culture, but on some occasions it is unnecessary to translate all the dynasties when there is no need to grasp every period depending on the situational context.

Example 5-2   ST: 山西五台山是闻名中外的佛教圣地，境内迄今仍保存着北魏、唐、宋、元、明、清及民国历朝历代的寺庙建筑 47 座，精美绝伦的古建艺术、稀世文物及博大雄宏的佛教文化充满了神秘感。

TT: On Wutai Mountain, located in Shanxi Province, there are 47 temples built during the seven dynasties from Northern Wei (386-534) to the Republic of China (1912-1949). Splendid ancient architecture, rare relics and unparalleled Buddhist culture have all lent mystery to the mountain.

(Jia Wenbo, 2004)

Wutai Mountain in China is a sacred Buddhist mountain boasting the temples and relics of Buddhist culture. There are 47 temples representing all dynasties' architectures ranging from the Northern Wei dynasty to the Republic of China. It is unnecessary to translate every dynasty into English since the meaning focus is put on the numerous temples. Given the context, the translator incorporated the

75

list of dynasties by briefly rendering the beginning and last period of the temples. This arrangement foregrounded the central idea and meanwhile demonstrated the translator's active manipulation on the version.

5.2   Deixis of Place

There is a sea of spatial references in the tourism text for introducing the geographical location of the scenic spots. They help the tourists identify the location of the tourist destination. In the English language, places are mainly in the form of prepositions (*in*, *on*, *to*, *behind*…), verb pairs (*come-go*, *bring-take*), adverbs (*here*, *there*) and place names (*New York, Niagara Falls*). Chinese spatial references share most of the features with the English language. One of the differences lies in the introduction of neighboring locations where variant prepositions are required. The choice of preposition is agitated to the Chinese translators in that the various English prepositions are much subtler than the Chinese counterparts.

Example 5-3   ST: 大明湖位于济南市区北部的大明湖公园，东、西、北三面接邻古城墙，南面紧靠市区，故赢得"城中之湖"的美誉。

TT: Located in the Daming Park in the north part of the city proper of Jinan, the Daming Lake adjoins the old city wall on the east, west and north and it is next to the city proper on the south, hence the title "an Inner-city Lake."

(Zhou Changjun & Zhang Zhongshui, 2004)

When introducing two separate locations, Chinese often use the prepositional phrases "在 …… 的东（西，南，北）面" or "在 …… 里面（外面）" no matter whether the two places are remote or near to each other. On the contrary, English has a special division of prepositions depending on the distance. If one place is in the domain of the other place, the preposition *in* will be taken up; if one place is near the border of the other, *on* will show up; if there is a long distance between them, *to* will direct the location. Daming Lake is located in the Daming Park that borders the old wall on all the sides. As a result, the prepositions *in* and *on* were employed accordingly. It had a long distance with the city proper, thus *to* was employed here. Correct translation on the preposition has a high significance to the tourism text due to the vast amount of location deixis in scenic spot introductions. Mistakes can be avoided if we distinguish the usages of preposition in mind.

Absolute spatial relations are dimensions as North-South and East-West. Two things should be noted in translation of absolute spatial relations in tourism text. One is the inversion in the inner part of the compounding Northeast, Northwest, Southeast and Southwest due to different collocation habits (For more details, refer to Chapter 3). The other is adding the absolute spatial references to position the stretching of the place for the foreign tourists, who will not get lost in the future traveling.

Example 5-4   ST: 湖上有彩带似的苏堤、白堤飘落其上。

TT: The Su Causeway which runs from north to south and the Bai Causeway which runs from east to west, look like two colored ribbons floating on the water.

(Lu Min, 2005)

The foreign tourists may confuse the Su Causeway with the Bai Causeway as they are similarly parallel causeways on the West Lake. To disambiguate the locations, the translator actively added absolute spatial references "from north to south" and "from east to west" to signify the stretching of the causeways. This active adaptation deepens tourists' geographical understanding on the causeways by relocating the position.

5.3   Deixis of Person

Person deixis is one of the ways by which a language is anchored into a context of use. The employment of the pronoun "you" is the most effective person deixis to show the host's hospitality in the tourism text. The use of "you," like carrying out a face-to-face conversation with the tourists, establishes a friendly and harmonious relationship between the host and the tourist. Thus it occurs frequently in Chinese and English tourism texts. Literal translation or addition of *you* in C-E or E-C tourism text translation will shorten the reader's psychological distance to the writer and strengthen their intimate relationship.

Example 5-5   ST: Pick a picnic lunch, bring along a good book, sit back and enjoy the views and delight in the splendor of this beautiful region.

TT: 带上野餐，再加上一本好书，舒舒服服坐下来好好欣赏一下这儿优美的景色，你会感到心旷神怡。

(Lu Min, 2005)

The source is an imperative sentence with four consecutive dynamic verbs to call on the tourists to travel in the place. To correspond to the appellative function of the source text, the translator added a personal deixis *you*, increasing the intimacy to the target readers. A harmonious relationship had been set up and laid good foundations for the future communication.

5.4   Requirements on the Translator

Adaptation to the physical world also means the material requirements to the translators. Translation is a decoding process from one language to the other language involving social, cultural and psychological correlates. Based on different guiding principles, it can be classified into theoretical translation and practical translation. As for qualified practical translators, they should be equipped with professional knowledge on a special field. A translator for Shakespearean sonnet must be a poet or have strong senses for poetry. Tourism text translators should get to know the basic concepts in tourism and other related fields such as tourist economics, management, laws and policies to shed light on the translation of tourism text. As for theoretical translators, they should be equipped with comprehensive bilingual knowledge on linguistic, cultural and social parameters. Furthermore, it is advisable to employ the adaptive translation techniques to convert the source text flexibly in order to be accepted by the target readers. All these material requirements on translators provide prerequisites for the successful translation activities.

Chapter 6
Adaptation to the Mental World in Tourism Text Translation

Xiao Longfu (2005) once conducted an interesting questionnaire on the reactions of foreign tourists to a sinking ship. The story said that when a large ship was about to go down, a lifeboat came quickly to rescue it. Seeing this, the English said, "We must keep a stiff upped lip!" The American said, "What a great experience!" The German responded, "This is the choice of life and death." When it came to the French, they cheered, "What a romantic scene!" We can learn from the story that different words to the same event reflect different psychology. English people are too conservative to show their scares even in danger. Americans are open and love ventures in their life and career. We can find clues in the American English dictionary, *venture* has double meanings. One defines an enterprise as a "Joint Venture" and the other means to have a risk. In American's mind, running an enterprise is like taking an adventure, both of which manifest the American adventurous soul. The same beliefs permeate in the American's daily life. However, Germans are serious and logical while Frenchmen are romantic, which contributes to the different reactions in face of disaster. In terms of tourism industry, different psychology leads to various consuming behaviors, and it is necessary for us to be aware of the tourists' mental world so as to guide for the translation. The mental world activated in language use contains cognitive and emotive elements.

American scholar John A. Thomas once proposed 18 motivations for outside traveling. Another American tourist professor W. Macintosh divided motivations into four types: bodily motivation, cultural motivation, communicative motivation and prestigious motivation. For the convenience of further investigation, the author categories tourists' motivations into four aspects.

Firstly, motivations for health. Modern life enables people to accumulate thousands of dollars as well as put on heavy stress. Some couldn't cope with such burdens that mental diseases like anxiety, fear, hollowness and depression have a detrimental effect on people's health. It is reported that many of the tourist consumers—office people, are on the verge of sub-health stage. People need to relax as a break or escape from the busy life. Going outside provides a better platform to relax both physically and mentally. In the course of traveling, one can ride a horse on the vast grassland, climb the gorgeous mountains on foot, or visit a temple/church to find the inner peace that the outside noisy world is not endowed with. Sighing at the wonderfulness and creativity of the nature, all the worries seem to go by. It is just for the benefit of physical and mental health that more and more people choose to go outside. At the same time, the comparatively lowered traveling expenses make traveling possible for the mass.

Secondly, motivations for interpersonal communication. Modern people are always on the move to seek for the suitable working conditions. One relationship hasn't been set up yet before they move to another place. After going home, people always feel hollow since they neglect to communicate with friends and neighbors in time. Things will change when people go outside. Especially in the countryside, local people are frugal and hospitable to entertain friends from all over the world. They offer their best food, show them around the village and give the tourists local dance at night. A harmonious atmosphere will accompany the tourists and give them much warmth during the whole journey. Besides, friendship is easily set up in traveling since there are no fundamental interest conflicts between the new acquaintances. Occasionally, when tourists cooperate to finish a difficult task (such as cross the desert, pongee), they will learn the teamwork spirit of helping each other out of difficulties and get the pleasure from the bottom of heart. This will benefit a lot for their future company work centering on the teamwork spirit. In a word, going outside eases tensions in interpersonal communication and harmonizes the interpersonal relationships by meeting with new friends.

Thirdly, motivations for self-improvement. People going outside are not only for relaxation and amusement, but also for acquiring knowledge. On the way to the destination, tourists will have more chances to get in touch with the local geography, architecture, habits, social customs, ways of life and so on. These brand new experiences will widen their horizon and supplement to the present ways of existence. Nowadays a lot of touring groups are instructive, especially for children. The recent popular "the Countryside Tour" and the "Red Tourism" familiarize the urban children with the countryside life and instruct them about the revolutionary life in the old days. By learning the pioneering life of the forefathers, children will cherish the present life and correct the old habits of being spoiled. In 2005, the theme tour "The Red Revolution Tour" brought people back to the hard revolutionary days for the establishment of People's Republic of China, which would educate the young to inherit the martyrs' wills and make our country strong and wealthy. Sightseeing contributes to people's self-improvement and does a lot of help for their growth.

Fourthly, motivations for assimilating the advanced science and technology and promoting the home culture. The first traveling activity in China dated back to the Western Han dynasty when Zhang Qian, a politician, has been to Xi Yu (ancient Western Region) twice and brought back seeds and medicine books. It sped up the transmission of western techniques in China. Ever since then, traveling as a way of assimilating advanced science and technology has been paid special attention. Today's world is a global village where no country can live alone. Cooperation has become the epochal theme at present days. For instance, the parts in a Boeing plane are produced by hundreds of different countries to ensure its taking off. Without cooperation, not a single plane can be produced. It is also for the cooperation with the advanced countries that developing countries have the possibility to grow fast. Under such circumstances, tourism flourishes as a means of cross-cultural communication to assimilate the advanced science and technology and publicize the home culture. People of developing countries go abroad to acquire the modern skills to return for the homeland, meanwhile experts in some special fields fly to other countries to impart the modern techniques. When the modern technologies are finally converted into productive force, people will be entitled to enjoy the fruits that tourism has brought about. In the context of "Chinese culture going global," travelling also provides a feasible means to enable foreign tourists to fully comprehend the Chinese culture.

6.1   The Aesthetic View of the Target Tourists

China boasts magnificent natural scenery and cultural relics in the course of 5,000 years of existence. The ancient temples, sacred mountains, bubbling rivers and so on leave a great impression on the tourists. In Chinese tourism text, Chinese usually use a great many rhetorical devices to sing high praise for their homeland. Therefore, dozens of poems, quotations and allusions increase the literariness of the text. A vivid translation on these poems would arouse the foreign tourists' resonance to the natural scenery.

Example 6-1   ST: 会当凌绝顶，一览众山小。

TT: I must ascend the mountain's crest;

It dwarfs all peaks under my feet.

(Xu Yuanchong, 2004)

The poem was composed by Chinese poet Du Fu to praise the marvelous Mount Taishan when he ascended the summit of the great mountain. Viewing panoramically from the summit, all the other mountains seemed lower and smaller, so the descendants called Mount Taishan "the Head of the Five Great Mountains (In China, Mount Taishan, Hengshan in Hunan Province, Huashan, Hengshan in Shanxi Province and Songshan are regarded as the Five Great Mountains)." Through this poem, the poet metaphorically expressed his ambitions to reach the summit in life and career. The translator used two formal verbs "ascend" and "dwarf" to highlight the social status that Mount Taishan was endowed with. Furthermore, the words "crest" and "feet" rhymed with the other lines in the poem by the feet /e/ and /iː/ respectively.

Chinese believe in "all in oneness." That is to say, they emphasize to harmonize with the nature and society. Harmony consists of healthy disagreements and democracy, respecting the interests of the individuals as well as the group. Chinese Yin and Yang, and the Five Elements (metal, wood, water, fire and earth) embody the harmony since each pair co-exist as well as contradict each other. The ancient Chinese palaces, halls and temples are designed with symmetrical structures. As for the style of tourism text, there are antithesis, parallelism and four-character phrases adding the symmetrical beauty of the Chinese language. Even a single Chinese character is filled with harmony no matter from what angle they are perceived. But it does not hold true for the English language. English people are influenced by utilitarian, which relies more on facts rather than intuition. When reading the tourism text, they wonder more about the number of scenic spots, the adventurous experience they may get and the comforting facilities in traveling. Therefore, the English tourism text is characterized by brevity with facts. Translators should change the format of languages to adapt to different aesthetic values.

Example 6-2   ST:（石门山）主峰海拔 406 米，峰峦叠嶂，泉水潺潺，洞壑幽深，古木苍翠，景色秀丽，有水雪洞、藤花幄灯二十四景，"石门月霁" 尤为胜景。

TT: Presenting pretty scenery of peaks upon peaks, murmuring streams, deep caves and verdant ancient trees, the Stone-Gate Mountain has 24 spots of interest such as "the Water-Snow Cave," "the Vine-Flower Curtain," of which the best-known one is "the Clear Moon Seen from the Stone-Gate Mountain."

(Zhou Changjun & Zhang Zhongshui, 2004)

The Chinese text has five parallel four-character phrases to portray the Stone-Gate Mountain as if unfolding a picturesque painting on the scenery. A word-for-word translation into English would be ponderous for the English readers. The translator instead simply listed the scenes with adjectives before them. This rendering seemed brief and powerful to coincide with the foreign tourists' aesthetic psychology.

6.2   The Different Thinking Patterns

6.2.1   Linear and Spiral

Chinese people are conservative. They are accustomed to beating about the bush before touching on the real topic. Their logic is like a whirling spiral centering around the major topic. However, the English are frank to speak out the truth when the conversation begins. People call their logic the linear type. This difference can be shown in the organization of tourism texts that Chinese usually reserve the focal point to the end while English people propose it as the topic sentence at the very beginning.

Example 6-3   ST: 在四川的西部,有一处奇妙的去处。它背倚岷山主峰雪宝顶, 树木苍翠,花香喜人,鸟声婉转,流水潺潺。它就是松潘县的黄龙。
TT: One of Sichuan's finest spots is Huanglong (Yellow Dragon), which lies in Songpan Mountain. It has lush green forests, filled with fragrant flowers, bubbling streams and song birds.

(Lu Min, 2005)

After a vivid description of the scenery, the Chinese source text aimed to create a suspense, so the topic sentence was put at the end of the paragraph. When converting the source, the translator put forward the topic sentence directly at the beginning of the paragraph, emphasizing the central ideas. This adaptation suited more with the foreign tourists' thinking patterns.

6.2.2   Dialectical Synthesis and Analytic Thinking

Traditionally speaking, Chinese usually conduct the dialectical synthesis to analyze the world. The central idea of dialectical thinking is whole and dynamic balance, etc. There are logical analysis in Chinese schools of thought, such as Confucius once proposed "Learning without thinking is useless. Thinking without learning is dangerous." Mencius argued "Thinking means attainment. No thinking means no attainment." The mainstream of Chinese thoughts is dialectical synthesis. Xiao Longfu (2005) pointed out that the ancient scholars advocated things as "a whole dynamic state, dialectical synthesis, and intuitional personal understanding." When it comes to the organization of the tourism text, Chinese unite the whole text by means of the embedded meaning. Their thought flows in a chronological or spatial order without explicit connecting devices to denote the relationship between the clauses. In addition, antithesis, parallelism and four-character phrases foreground the symmetrical beauty of languages. But that is not applicable to the English language. English people value more on natural sciences. They are dominated by the logical thinking rather than intuition. Therefore, there are a lot of discourse markers, present and past participles and prepositional phrases to signify the logical and temporal relationship between the ingredients. Adding the cohesive devices to the English target text is elementary to Chinese translators. For further details, the readers may refer to Example 4-8.

Chapter 7
Adaptation to the Social World
in Tourism Text Translation

Social factors play a significant role in language communication. The semantics, syntax and style in language use are all influenced by the social correlates, most of which are social settings or institutions. Social factors will confine the rules of communication in which certain types of linguistic acts can be performed. Social institutions, for instance, will empower the superior to command, order and request while the inferior has to obey the orders. Other social ingredients such as culture, religion, politics, ethics, histories, geography, age, sex and education will more or less shape the social practice. Due to divergent social backgrounds, people of different nations may hold different views on the same thing. For example, a chrysanthemum in China can symbolize uprightness, longevity and purity. But in Japan it means to mourn for the dead. Translators should adapt to the requirements of different social world especially the taboos and make necessary changes if possible.

7.1　The Sociocultural Background

As the functions of tourism texts are the information conveyance and cultural transmission, cultural ingredients are embodied hither and thither in the tourism text.

Misunderstandings may arise if the translator does not notice the cultural variances between the source and target texts.

Example 7-1　　ST: 怡红院

　　　　　　　TT1: the House of Red Delights

　　　　　　　TT2: the House of Green Delights

(Yang Hsien-yi & Yang Gladys, 2015)

"Red" in the Chinese context is a favorite national color which symbolizes revolution, hospitality and everlasting happiness. When foreign ministers pay visits to China, they all step on the red carpet which signifies the warmest welcome. When getting married, the bride loves to wear red clothes in wish for propitious omens. When the spring festival draws near, people put up the red spring couplets on the gate to wish for health and good harvest in the coming year. "Red" in China also connotes revolution. The flying red flag reminds people of the honorable martyrs who had sacrificed their lives for the establishment of the People's Republic of China. However, "red" in the English countries is regarded as brutal since it is the symbol of blood. The "house" in the source text is a working and resting apartment for an energetic and talented young fellow Jia Baoyu, so a literal translation of "red" will contradict the meaning. Therefore, the translator rewrote the source text with the word "green" which in English symbolized the vibrancy of the people. Such an active adaptation highlighted the juvenile protagonist with the equivalent pragmatic effects in the source text.

Numbers can connote different cultural meanings as well. The number "seven" enjoys high reputation in the Western countries. For instance, Christian doctrines hold that God spent seven days to create the world. Greek vow to say "to come under the influence of seven things." Apart from these, there are the seven virtues, the seven deadly sins and the seven heavens, etc. The marvelous wonders of the world are seven too, including the Pyramids of Egypt, the Hanging Gardens of Babylon, the tomb of Mausolus, the Temple of Diana at Ephesus, the Colossus of Rhodes, the Statue of Jupiter by Phidias and the Pharos of Alexandria. "Seven" is endowed with such a sacred power in the Western countries that people show great respect to it. On the contrary, Chinese prefer to the number *nine* because in the Chinese legends, it stands for the infinite universe extended into holiness. With the homonyms " 久 " (means permanent), the number expresses people's wishes to last forever. Emperors try every means to connect themselves with the number to show how holy and inviolable they are. In Chinese mythology, the heaven is divided into nine layers. Emperors pay pilgrimages to the mountains nine times a year. Halls, pavilions and chambers are constructed in nine courtyards in Confucius Mansions. The number *nine* also receives high popularity from the ordinary people in that it expresses wishes for stability and longevity. The lunar November 9th in China is celebrated as "the Old Men's Day" in the hope of a long lifespan for the old. In terms of Chinese tourism text, the number *nine* appears from time to time when related to the mountains, temples, halls and stories.

Example 7-2   ST: 齐烟九点坊

TT1: the Archway for Viewing the Nine Hills (Zhou Changhun, 2004)

TT2: the Archway for Viewing the Nine Hills of Qi County in the Mist (The number *nine* in Chinese culture is a popular void denotation to infinity)

(TT2 is translated by the author)

The archway is named after the poem composed by Li He, a Chinese poet of the Tang dynasty. It was read as " 遥望齐州九点烟 ," which depicted the nine hills located in the northern outskirts of Jinan. Looking afar, the nine hills were vaguely visible in the morning smoke and evening mist just like the clouds. Nine hills here did not necessarily mean there were actually nine hills but a vague denotation since it was hard to count on the hills in the mist. *Nine* in the Chinese context is welcomed by all walks of life as a popular void denotation to significance and infinity. The choice of *nine* reflected the poet's psychological preference for the number in that it associated the readers with the remoteness of the hills by looking afar. Free translation is a good choice, but could it be better rendering when adding the background information *"Nine* in Chinese culture is a void denotation for infinity?"

In the questionnaire the author conducted, this version got the highest marks because it was "cultural, vivid and proper."

7.2 The Social Norms

China evolves from a feudal agricultural society in which the patriarchal clan system maintained the social orders. There were strict regulations between father and son, husband and wife and king and minister where Chinese thought highly of blood relationship and hierarchy. It was a bit hard for a man of humble birth to succeed without blood ties. In interpersonal communication, people usually call each other the official title to indicate the social status. When traveling around China, one may see gorgeous palaces, pavilions and halls representing the emperors' mighty power. In Qufu of Shandong Province, no architecture is permitted to be higher than the Confucius Mansion, implying that nobody exceeds the achievements that Confucius has made. When having dinner, etiquette rules as well. The table is designed squarely, displaying the old Chinese belief "The heaven is round and the earth is square." The old or the superior will be seated directly facing the door and others sit around him/her according to age, sex and social status. The nearer people sit to the old, the higher status they have. In English tourism text, personal self-amusement activities such as comforting facilities, exciting adventure experience will lure tourists to pay a visit. Translators should pay much attention to the different requirements of social norms on the language choices. Adaptive strategies can be employed to amend the cultural loss.

Example 7-3　ST: 宫墙内，建筑物有 110 多处，宫、殿、馆、斋、楼、台、亭、榭，多如群星。

TT: Within the wall, there are more than 110 architectural structures, including palaces, studies and outbuildings for work and daily life, and towers, terraces, summerhouses and pavilions for landscaping purposes, scattered all over the villa like stars in the sky.

(Lu Naisheng & Jin Yingying, 2000)

Eight classical Chinese architectures in the source may be puzzling to the foreign tourists with no adequate cultural background information. To make it clear, the translator categorized all the architectures into two types—for work and daily life and for landscaping purposes. This arrangement clarifies the pragmatic social functions each building plays and will be easily recognized by the foreign tourists.

7.2.1 Religion

Early in the feudal society, Chinese kings advocated Confucianism, Taoism and Buddhism to consolidate their sovereignty. Up till now, the three religions have inserted such a great impact on the Chinese society that some of the doctrines have become the moral standards to guide behaviors. Every year, millions of believers pay visit to the temples to show their respect. On the contrary, Christianity is popular in the Western countries. Saturdays and Sundays are considered as holy resting time for a peaceful mind in the church. Those religions have strikingly different doctrines and values on life. For instance, Confucius once proposed "Harmony is not the sameness," which laid foundation for dealing with the conflicts. Chinese classic architectures, such as halls, palaces and temples, are constructed symmetrically to symbolize the harmonious beauty. In dealing with interpersonal relationship, harmony is regarded as the guiding principle to be tolerant of the disagreements. On the contrary, the essence of Christianity is self-fulfillment. One of the typical Western architectures is the Gothic built in the 12th to 16th century characterized by pointed arches, clusters of columns, etc. The pointed arches straightly lead to the sky, demonstrating the Christian doctrine of personal struggle for self-fulfillment in heaven after death. Therefore, translators need to actively add the necessary background information to adapt to the religious setting in the target readers.

Example 7-4   ST: 大足石刻是东方三教合一的艺术宫殿。

TT: The stone carvings of Dazu are the art palace of the oriental combination of the three religions—Confucianism, Buddhism and Taoism.

(Lu Naisheng & Jin Yingying, 2000)

In the English-speaking countries, Christianity and Protestant are two dominant religions to guide people's spiritual life. However, Chinese people believe in Confucianism, Buddhism and Taoism within the evolution of time, which have different doctrines from the foreign countries. Therefore, the author explained the three religions in detail to make the versions clearer to the foreign tourists.

7.2.2 Geography

China is situated in a semi-closed continental region with the Pacific Ocean to the east. The comforting east wind from the ocean brings about the coolness in the hot summer, thus the east wind is popularly received in the Chinese culture. When everything is ready except one key point, people often say " 万事俱备, 只欠东风 ", which literally means we lack only the east wind of luck. That is not the case in the Western countries. They are located alongside the Mediterranean Ocean where the west wind is much enjoyable. British poet Shelley (1792-1822) once wrote a poem "Ode to the West Wind" to express appreciation for the west wind. Translators should flexibly adapt the versions to the different geographical settings.

Example 7-5   ST: (a slogan on the Dai Temple in Mount Taishan) 紫气东来

TT: the Noble Wind from the West

(Translated by the author)

The purple color in the Chinese context symbolizes the noble and superior and the east direction is the place where luck and chances are generated. The slogan is posted to the east side of the Dai Temple in Shandong Province implying that the noble men will be born of the east. This pragmatic effect was conveyed by the west wind in the English countries. To achieve the functional equivalence, the author changed the source into "the noble wind from the west" in accordance with the target geographical settings. 56.7% of the English-major postgraduates voted for the version.

7.2.3 Histories and Politics

History shapes who we are, where we go and what we do. "Forgetting the past means betrayal." There are cooperation as well as struggles between the countries in the course of the historical evolvement. Translators should protect their national interests and sovereignty as well as respect other Western countries' laws and social regulations. Taiwan has always been an inseparable part of China since the ancient times. However, some Western countries don't acknowledge it by separating Taiwan from the mainland as an independent country. In the world maps issued by Google Earth, Taiwan was once wrongly marked as a country with its capital. Every Chinese translator has the responsibility to correct this huge mistake. At the same time, when a period of history is unknown to the foreign tourists, translators can strategically introduce it to the tourists by special techniques.

Example 7-6   ST: 北京故宫耗时 14 年，整个工程于 1420 年结束。

TT1: The construction of the Forbidden City took 14 years, and was finished in 1420, 14 years before Shakespeare was born.

TT2 :... in 1420, 72 years before Christopher Columbia discovered the New World.

(Ye Miao, 2005)

The year 1420 is memorable for the Chinese since in that year the magnificent Forbidden City was constructed while English tourists might have a vague idea on it. The translator then compared it to the event time when the greatest literary figure Shakespeare was born or Columbia discovered the New World. Meanwhile, different versions were chosen according to the different target readers. When it came to the English tourists, the first version would be chosen; as for the American tourists, the second would be adopted. By using this analogy, tourists would recognize easily its significance in the Chinese history.

7.3   Adaptation to the Readers' Feedback

Language is changing with time and tide. Propelled by modern science and technology, new words and phrases are created to satisfy the needs of daily communication whereas out-of-dated usages are crossed out. In terms of translation, there are unconventional phrases and collocations in the versions hampering readers' flow of thought. Meanwhile, people's appreciation for good versions is improving as a result of changes on language property and sociocultural settings. Let's take the Bible translation as an example. The English version for the Bible in the Renaissance period was regarded as the classics at that time, but as time went by, different versions sprung up to be in compatible with the tastes of people in different times. As is held by Newmark (2001), translation is to "produce on its readers an effect as close as possible to that obtained on the readers of the original." Consequently, readers' reactions to the original versions are the key parameters to assess the versions' quality. Questionnaire and interview may be conducted on whether the versions can be accepted by the domestic and foreign tourists. In the tide of "Chinese culture going abroad", translators should not only pay more attention to the feedback of the target readers, but also retain the cultural uniqueness.

In conclusion, given that tourism text translation is adaptation to the source texts' structure and communicative context, the author proposes her model of tourism text translation. See Figure 7-1.

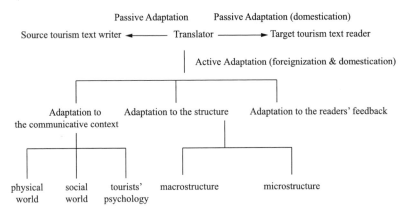

Figure 7-1　Adaptation Translation Model for Tourism Text

Translators as a bridge connecting source tourism text writers and target readers take the initiatives in two layers of conversion. The first occurs between source tourism text writer and translator where the translator passively adapts to the linguistic, cognitive and social environment by comprehending the explicit and implicit meanings the source text conveys. In the second period, the translator converts both passively and actively what he/she has got from the source to the target tourism text. Passive adaptation signifies that the translator should respect the sociocultural norms in the target text without any alterations. The tourism text intends to provide tourists with information on the destination and spread culture to the outside world. In order to produce the same effects on the target readers as the source text to the source readers, domestication translation skills are employed to meet with the cognition of the target tourism text readers. Active adaptation refers to the translators' selection on word choice, syntax, style and discourse when facing a lot of choices in translation. It enables translators to pick out the most appropriate and idiomatic versions to the source text. The subjectivity of the translators in translation process is fully demonstrated in this period. Foreignization and domestication translation skills are generally taken up by translators in order to transmit the Chinese culture to the outside world or render the version more idiomatic.

In the course of tourism text translation, translators adapt to the target texts' structure, communicative context and readers' feedback. Structure can be subdivided into macrostructure like the discourse and microstructure like word choice, syntax and style. Communicative context refers to adaptation to the tourists' physical world, social world and psychology. The ability to properly handle the cultural-loaded ingredients will affect the version's acceptability by the target readers. Meanwhile, translators should pay attention to the readers' feedback to the version and ready to revise it in that it reflects the qualities of the version in a lateral way and will affect the future tourist promotion. Furthermore, translation is a dynamic process giving varied demands on translators as time goes by; therefore, the standard of adaptation to those factors is changing with time to suit with different tourists' tastes.

Chapter 8
Translation Strategies for
Tourism Text Translation

People travel for different purposes. Some are eager to experience the colorful alien culture, while others are for relaxation or a break of the routine life. This leads to the variant demands on the tourism text versions. Foreign tourists wish the versions either easy to follow or filled with cultural specifics. Therefore, active and passive adaptation translation strategies are adopted to compensate for the linguistic, social, mental and cultural losses. Here adaptation specifically means the adaptation to the target readers. Passive adaptation strategies show translators' respect to the target texts' linguistic, cultural, social and psychological norms without alterations. As a result, domestication method is mainly adopted to be in fit with the target readers' sociocultural background. Active adaptation strategies manifest translators' active manipulation on word choice, syntax, style and discourse. Translators can either adapt to the source text to promote the source culture, or adapt to the target readers to gain acceptance of the version. In this case, translators can combine foreignization with domestication translation methods to publicize the Chinese culture or render the version more idiomatic. Specifically speaking, the passive and active adaptation translation strategies in the tourism text can be manifested as follows.

8.1   Transliteration

Transliteration is the translation of the cultural-loaded Chinese scenic spots by use of Chinese Pinyin. It will foreground the Chinese specialties in order to be appreciated and accepted by foreign tourists.

Example 8-1   ST: 福娃

TT: Fuwa

Fuwa was chosen as the mascot of Beijing Olympic Games in 2008, demonstrating the Chinese specialties to the whole world. It consists of typical Chinese culture-loaded cartoon characters of a fish (called Beibei), panda (Jingjing), Olympic Flame (Huanhuan), Tibetan antelope (Yingying) and swallow (Nini). Panda is Chinese national treasure. Tibet is an inseparable territory of China, and swallow in the Chinese context symbolizes swiftness and happiness. The five mascots are connected by the Olympic ring which symbolizes the China's unity with the world. Furthermore, the five hues of Olympic rings stand for the five elements in nature—sea, forest, fire, earth and sky. Besides, they are made up of clay since China is famous for clay dolls. As is held by the designer, Han Meilin, "Wearing animal-shape hats can best link our traditional dolls with the existing drafts." With so much Chinese culture embedded in the mascots, the best way to translate them is employing a typical Chinese way—Chinese Pinyin. That is the reason why the transliteration Fuwa is finally set up after months of negotiation.

Correct transliteration of place names should be paid special attention since they concern about the territorial issues of China. When it comes to place names with one monosyllabic plus one monosyllabic general term, transliteration of the two syllabus plus a free translation of the general name is preferred. Especially when lost in the way, pronouncing the transliteration will be easily recognized by the local people and lead the tourists to the destination because they sound similar to the Chinese equivalences.

Example 8-2　泰山 Mount Taishan

尼山 Mount Nishan

庐山 Mount Lushan

Otherwise, when the names of the scenic spots are comprised of two of more specific syllabus plus a general monosyllabic place name, the transliteration of the place is replaced by a combination of transliteration and free translation methods.

Example 8-3　刘公岛 the Liugong Island

徂徕山 Mount Culai

蒲松龄故居　Former Residence of Pu Songling

When it comes to Chinese territory, translators should remain alert and keep the political correctness. For instance, the place "钓鱼岛"（literally mean fishing island), an inseparable territory of China, should be rendered as "Diaoyu Island" instead of the Japanese versions.

8.2　Addition

The cultural-loaded words may harass the foreign tourists for lack of corresponding cultural knowledge. In this case, adding the necessary background information will compensate for the cultural losses in communication. Footnote, endnote, dashes, brackets and explanation are common techniques for tourism text translation.

Example 8-4　ST: 济南诞生了许多历史上的著名人物，像中医科学的奠基人扁鹊，阴阳五行学派大师邹衍，唐代开国元勋房玄龄、秦琼，中国著名文学家李清照、辛弃疾等。

TT: In Chinese history, Jinan gave birth to a number of famous figures, such as Bian Que (the founder of the science of traditional Chinese medicine), Zou Yan (a great master of the theories of Yin & Yang and the Five Elements—metal, wood, water, fire and earth—

whose theories were used by ancient Chinese philosophers to explain the origin of the world), Fang Xuanling and Qin Qiong (the founding fathers of the Tang dynasty), and Li Qingzhao and Xin Qiji (two outstanding Chinese literati).

(Information Office of Jinan Municipal People's Government, 2005)

Foreign readers may be unfamiliar with the Chinese figures in Jinan's history. The translator then adapted to the foreign tourists' sociocultural world by using brackets to explain the figures. Meanwhile, the content of the Five Elements was added to make the foreign tourists fully aware of the Chinese culture. Other techniques like incorporation when adding information rendered the version brief and logical.

8.3   Deletion

Deletion is crossing out the redundant ingredients to project the central ideas in the text. As far as the Chinese tourism text is concerned, adjectives, four-character phrases, quotations and repetition may be ponderous for the Westerners and hamper their understandings on the scenic spots. As a result, deleting the deviant information in translation will highlight the topics.

Example 8-5   ST: 祖国山水,风格多样:多样的风格,相对应而存在,相比较而多姿。杭州西湖,水榭歌台,人工赋予它典雅美。蜀中仙山峨嵋,漂浮于云涛雾海,呈秀色于烟雨浸漫的山林。誉满中华的桂林山水,水秀山奇,山水平分秋色。

TT: China is a land of scenic contrasts, each uniquely representing its own area: West Lake in Hangzhou with enchanting pavilions set in quiet surroundings, Mount Emei in Sichuan with peaks peeping through mist and clouds, Guilin in Guangxi with panoramic views of mountains and rivers.

(Bi Fengzhou, 1985)

The source text was elegantly written to form a parallel structure, which was a custom in Chinese tourism writing but maybe regarded as hypocritical by the foreign tourists. Repetition and antithesis were employed by the source writer to increase the symmetric beauty. A literal translation carried on too much mental processing on the foreign tourists. The translator, instead, incorporated the original three sentences into one sentence by deleting the repetitious words. For instance, the repetitious " 山秀山奇，山水平分秋色 " that literally means the similarly charming mountain and water landscape were deleted and replaced by an adjective "panoramic." Such rendering adapted to foreign readers' requirements on information and brevity.

8.4 Analogy

Analogy is a kind of metaphor which compares the unknown things to the familiar ones. It is commonly practiced in tourism text translation because the version will be easily comprehended by the foreign tourists. Because of cultural variances, a literal translation will not meet with tourists' need of the cultural background information. However, an analogy will render the version clear and vivid to the foreign tourists.

Example 8-6   ST: 大雁塔位于西安南郊大慈恩寺境内，距市中心约 4 公里，是我国佛教名塔之一。

TT: Situated in Da Ci'en Temple (the Temple of Thanksgiving), about four kilometers south from the urban center, the Big Wild Goose Pagoda is one of the famous Buddhist Pagodas in China.

(Yao Baorong et al., 2004)

Da Ci'en Temple was constructed in AD 648 by Emperor Li Zhi in the Tang dynasty in memory of his late mother who had devoted all her love to the son. It is said that the Emperor would knee down on the temple every morning and night to thank for the great mother's nurture. When translating the name of the temple, the translator creatively compared it to thanksgiving—a festival in the Western countries to express gratitude to the American Indians who taught them how to survive in the harsh environment. With this analogy, the foreign tourists would easily grasp the cultural connotation embedded in the name.

There are other analogies in tourism text translation. For instance, "济公" (Ji Gong) can be compared to Chinese Robin Hood, the Beauty Xizi is regarded as Chinese Cleopatra, "梁祝"(Liang Shanbo & Zhu Yingtai) are named as Chinese Romeo and Juliet.

8.5 Adaptation

Chinese tourism texts differ greatly from the English texts as a result of readers' different linguistic, psychological and cultural habits. Chinese usually express their appreciation for the natural beauty by use of four-character phrases, repetition, metaphor and other devices in Chinese texts, which may be ponderous to the foreign tourists who value brevity. To achieve pragmatic equivalence, the translator can adapt the original source text to a simple one suitable for the foreign tourists. The same holds true for the English-to-Chinese translation.

Example 8-7   ST: 泉水清澈见底，水石相激，淙淙有声，犹如漱玉。

TT: The clear spring water is gurgling against the rocks just like rinsing the jade.

(Zhou Changjun & Zhang Zhongshui, 2004)

Four four-character phrases in the source functioning as parallelism increase the elegance and vigor of the text. However, its literal translation is not acceptable for the English readers because English focuses more on facts than intuition. The translator instead adapted the source to a simple sentence with a prepositional phrase, which coincided with the target readers' linguistic and psychological requirements on brevity. On special occasions, the translator may change the whole sentence patterns in accordance with the pragmatic effects.

Example 8-8   ST: 没去过海底世界，别说到过青岛。

TT: Welcome to the Qingdao Underwater World!

(From a slogan on Qingdao Underwater World)

Qingdao in Shandong Province is a coastal city boasting clear sky and blue sea. It has attracted millions of tourists especially after the 2008 Olympic Games. Its moderate climate, amusement facilities and Western architectural complex make Qingdao an ideal place for living. The source text can be understood as an adverbial clause of condition meaning that if one doesn't go to Underwater World, he/she can't claim to have been to Qingdao. In this case, Underwater World has become a cultural symbol of Qingdao. Or the slogan can be interpreted as an adverbial clause of cause-and-effect: because one doesn't go to the Underwater World, he/she can't claim to have been to Qingdao. This pejorative interpretation would leave an uncomfortable impression on the tourists. To avoid the ambiguity, the source flexibly took a pragmatic approach by using an imperative clause "Welcome to the Qingdao Underwater World!" to extend hospitality to the foreign friends. This rendering will be well received by the foreign tourists.

Chapter 9
Conclusion

9.1 The Research Rationale

The present thesis explored the adaptability in tourism text translation. Assuming that tourism text translation was a comprehensive conversion involving structural, physical, mental and social correlates, the author carried out her research from the perspective of Adaptation Theory and proposed the translation strategies. In terms of methodology, the study was a combination of qualitative and quantitative analysis. The corpus that the author used in this thesis came from those sources: the pictorials, tourist guide, pamphlets and public signs issued by the government, tourist bureau, travel agency and internet.

To testify the feasibility of applying Adaptation Theory to tourism text translation, the author conducted a survey on translation of scenic spots located mainly in Shandong Province to investigate how the correlates were taking effects in tourism text translation. Most of the results were compatible with the author's expectancy, making prerequisites for exploring tourism text translation in a pragmatic perspective. Then under the framework of Adaptation Theory, the author specified adaptation to the above correlates in tourism text translation by use of bilingual translation materials. As for the structural adaptation, the author studied it from the macro and micro angles. Macrostructure adaptation focused attention on the scope of a paragraph while microstructure adaptation laid emphasis on the sentential levels where lexical, syntactic, phonetic and stylistic adaptation strategies coincided with the grammatical limitation of the target texts. Then adaptation to the communicative context in the tourism text was manifested in the physical, mental and social correlates during the translation process. These ingredients were of much importance in tourism text translation in that they took on the responsibility of transmitting the home culture to the destination. Furthermore, proper handling of those ingredients would more or less influence the generation of the structures. Based on the above analysis, the author proposed her adaptation translation model in tourism text under the guidance of Adaptation Theory.

At the end of the thesis, the author put forward passive and active adaptive translation strategies guided by the model, such as transliteration, addition, omission, analogy and adaptation. Translators' subjectivity and manipulation on words were getting into full play in accordance with the readers' cognitive and sociocultural settings.

Taking the thesis as a whole, the author has four creative points in tourism text translation. Firstly, she proposed a new adaptive translation model, which would have a great significance in both translation theory and practice. She also found that tourism text translation was a multi-dimensional conversion adaptive to the target texts' structural, physical, mental and social worlds as well as readers' feedback to the versions. Thus, translators could consciously employ active and passive translation strategies like transliteration, addition, deletion and adaptation to mend for the cultural losses. Lastly, the author added that adaptation should also take the readers' feedback into account. The dynamic language property and variant sociocultural settings contributed to people's different appreciation for the same version at different periods. As a result, the author conducted the survey to test the acceptability of the versions. Readers' feedback is an effective tool to assess the versions' quality.

9.2   Implications of the Thesis

This model has greater implications both in translation methodology and translation teaching. Firstly, passive and active adaptation methods can provide a new perspective on translation strategy including the dichotomies among literal and free translation, covert and overt translation and domestication and foreignization. Wang Jianguo (2005) postulated that "Literal translation, free translation, domestication and foreignization are all translation methods." Applying both passive and active adaptation methods contributes to comprehend the ongoing translation process, avoiding the harassment of having to choose the alternative between two opposing methods.

Secondly, this model provides an operable and efficient way to translate the tourism text. As tourism text translation is an encompassing dynamic process, few systematic or thorough researches on tourism text translation have been conducted until now. However, this model has given a detailed framework to operate tourism text translation.

Thirdly, this model will guide for translation of different text types, such as translation of advertisement, contract and literary works. Different translation strategies like transliteration, addition, deletion and adaptation will be taken up according to the adaptive requirements of the target texts.

Last but not the least, this model will shed light on tourism text translation teaching. As indicated by the survey, most of the students are equipped with linguistic competence, but few of them are familiar with the mental and sociocultural environment of the target readers. Teachers thus can purposefully impart the destination's geographical, historical and cultural background knowledge to the students in class to make up for the cultural losses, making students aware of the importance of cultural background knowledge in language learning. In addition, teachers can ask students to read extensively after class to widen their horizon.

9.3　Limitations of the Thesis

In this thesis, the author mainly adopted a qualitative approach to investigate how the comprehensive correlates were taking effects in tourism text translation. A survey was attached to prove the author's point of view. However, the research method seemed to be unitary which needed to be further improved by other empirical research methods such as an interview. The subjects of the survey were mainly Chinese college students, and the author didn't test the acceptability of the versions by the foreign tourists. With the advancement of modern technology, tourism texts will be displayed through the multimedia, such as tourism texts with the pictures, the urban documentary or TikTok. Therefore, more attention will be paid to the multi-modal translation of tourism texts in the future.

References

[1]   Castello, Eric. *Tourist-Information Texts: a Corpus-Based Study of Four Related Genres*[M]. Padova: Unipress, 2002.

[2]   Connor, Ulla: *Contrastive Rhetoric: Cross-cultural Aspects of Second-language Writing*[M]. Shanghai: Shanghai Foreign Language Education Press, 2001.

[3]   Dalgish, Gerard M. *Webster's Dictionary of American English*[M]. Beijing: Foreign Language Teaching and Research Press, 1997.

[4]   Gandin, Stefania. Translating the Language of Tourism: A Corpus-Based Study on the Translational Tourism English Corpus (T-TourEC) [J]. *Procedia-Social and Behavioral Sciences*, 2013 (95): 325-335.

[5]   Gilbert, D. C. Government Intervention in the Marketing of Tourism Products[J]. *International Journal of Public Sector Management*, 1990 (02): 17-25.

[6]   Gutt, Ernest-August. *Translation and Relevance: Cognition and Context*[M]. Shanghai: Shanghai Foreign Language Education Press, 2004.

[7]   House, Juliane. *A Model for Translation Quality Assessment*[M]. Tübingen: Gunter Narr, 1981.

[8]   Hsien-yi Yang & Yang Gladys. *The Dream of Red Mansions*[M]. Beijing: Foreign Languages Press, 2015.

[9]   Morris, Charles W. *Foundations of the Theory of Signs*[M]. Chicago: The University of Chicago Press, 1938.

[10] Newmark, Peter. *A Textbook of Translation*[M]. London: Prentice Hall, 2001.

[11] Nida, Eugene & Taber, Charles. *The Theory and Practice of Translation* [M]. Shanghai: Shanghai Foreign Language Education Press, 2004.

[12] Nord, Christiane. *Translating as a Purposeful Activity: Functionalist Approaches Explained*[M]. Shanghai: Shanghai Foreign Language Education Press, 2001.

[13] Rojo, Luisa Martin. The Jargon of Delinquents and the Study of Conversational Dynamics [J]. *Journal of Pragmatics*, 1994(21): 243-289.

[14] Sperber, Dan & Wilson, Deindre. *Relevance: Communication and Cognition* [M]. Beijing: Foreign Language Teaching and Research Press, 2001.

[15] Verschueren, Jef. *Understanding Pragmatics*[M]. Beijing: Foreign Language Teaching and Research Press, 2000.

[16] 安春平,张治中,邢兆梅. 旅游文本的符号学翻译研究 [J]. 大连理工大学学报(社会科学版),2005(1): 89-92.

[17] 白蓝. 外宣翻译中的源语顺应 [J]. 外国语文,2018,34(5): 24-29.

[18] 包惠南. 文化语境与语言翻译 [M]. 北京:中国对外翻译出版公司,2001.

[19] 包惠南,包昂. 中国文化与汉英翻译 [M]. 北京:外文出版社,2004.

[20] 毕凤洲. 神话世界九寨沟 [M]. 成都:四川人民出版社,1985.

[21] 曹丹. 跨文化视野下的中国世界文化遗产研究及其意义 [D]. 成都:四川师范大学(硕士论文),2005.

[22] 陈代球. 汉语旅游文本中文化负载及意象的翻译:功能翻译观 [D]. 广州:广东外语外贸大学(硕士论文),2005.

[23] 陈刚. 旅游翻译与涉外导游 [M]. 北京:中国对外翻译出版公司,2004.

[24] 陈雯. 桂林旅游材料翻译的文化分析 [D]. 桂林:广西师范大学(硕士论文),2005.

[25] 陈向明. 质的研究方法与社会科学研究 [M]. 北京:教育科学出版社,2000.

[26] 高晖. 从顺应论的角度看中英广告的翻译 [D]. 广州:广东外语外贸大学(硕士论文),2004.

[27] 高云,韩丽. 语用翻译当属交际翻译 [J]. 西安外国语学院学报,2004,12(1): 45-47.

[28] 顾树森. 人间天堂杭州 [M]. 杭州:浙江人民出版社,2001.

[29] 戈玲玲. 顺应论对翻译研究的启示——兼论语用翻译标准 [J]. 外语学

刊, 2002(3): 7-11.

[30] 贾文波. 应用翻译功能论 [M]. 北京: 中国对外翻译出版公司, 2004.

[31] 纪爱梅. 齐鲁旅游文化的翻译 [D]. 济南: 山东师范大学(硕士论文), 2002.

[32] 济南市人民政府新闻办公室编.《中国济南》宣传册 [M]. 北京: 五洲传播出版社, 2005.

[33] 金惠康. 跨文化旅游翻译 [M]. 北京: 中国对外翻译出版公司, 2006.

[34] 鞠玉梅. 英语文体学 [M]. 青岛: 青岛海洋大学出版社, 1999.

[35] 康宁. 从语篇功能看汉语旅游语篇的翻译 [J]. 中国翻译, 2005(3): 85-89.

[36] 寇海珊. 基于目的论的旅游翻译充分性研究 [D]. 兰州: 西北师范大学(硕士论文), 2010.

[37] 李成团. 电视访谈"问答句"中"附加信息"的语用顺应之探究 [D]. 广州: 广东外语外贸大学(硕士论文), 2006.

[38] 李艳. 广告语对受众心理的动态顺应——一项基于中文女性化妆品广告的研究 [D]. 广州: 广东外语外贸大学(硕士论文), 2006.

[39] 李一楠. 旅游文本材料英译策略研究 [D]. 成都: 四川大学(硕士论文), 2005.

[40] 李晓光. 顺应论与社会指示 [D]. 哈尔滨: 黑龙江大学(硕士论文), 2005.

[41] 刘德军. 从文化语境的角度看旅游资料的翻译 [D]. 长沙: 湖南师范大学(硕士论文), 2006.

[42] 刘亮星. 架设文化沟通的桥梁——从目的论角度探索旅游文献的汉英翻译 [D]. 广州: 广东外语外贸大学(硕士论文), 2006.

[43] 刘坪. 法庭应答语的顺应性研究 [D]. 广州: 广东外语外贸大学(硕士论文), 2003.

[44] 卢敏. 英语笔译实务(2级)[M]. 北京: 外文出版社, 2005.

[45] 陆乃圣, 金颖颖. 英文导游词实用教程 [M]. 上海: 华东理工大学出版社, 2000.

[46] 马金凤. 旅游资料翻译探讨 [D]. 上海: 上海海运学院(硕士论文), 2003.

[47]　马萧．话语标记语的语用功能与翻译 [J]．中国翻译，2003（5）：38-41.

[48]　彭娟．英语重复的顺应性研究 [D]．长沙：湖南师范大学（硕士论文），2005.

[49]　青岛市人民政府新闻办公室编．青岛指南 [M]．青岛：青岛出版社，2002.

[50]　钱锺书．围城 [M]．北京：人民文学出版社，1991.

[51]　秦海涛．汉语反语的顺应性研究 [D]．广州：广东外语外贸大学（硕士论文），2006.

[52]　山东省人民政府新闻办公室编．《中国山东》宣传册 [M]．北京：五洲传播出版社，2006.

[53]　宋志平．翻译：选择与顺应——语用顺应论视角下的翻译研究 [J]．中国翻译，2004（3）：19-23.

[54]　苏冰．从文化翻译观谈中国旅游文本的英语翻译 [D]．济南：山东大学（硕士论文），2005.

[55]　王建国．从语用顺应论的角度看翻译策略与方法 [J]．外语研究，2005（4）：55-59.

[56]　王治奎．大学汉英翻译教程 [M]．济南：山东大学出版社，2002.

[57]　王晓元．性别、女性主义与文学翻译 [M]// 杨自俭．英汉语比较与翻译（4）．上海：上海外语教育出版社，2002：618-630.

[58]　文军，邓春，辜涛等．信息与可接受度的统一——对当前旅游翻译的一项调查与分析 [J]．中国科技翻译，2002（1）：49-52.

[59]　文月娥，周小玲．功能对等论与商标翻译 [J]．湘潭师范学院学报，2005（4）：100-102.

[60]　文月娥．从功能对等论看中式菜谱的英译 [J]．湘潭师范学院学报，2006：117-118.

[61]　翁凤翔．实用翻译 [M]．杭州：浙江大学出版社，2002.

[62]　吴亚欣，于国栋．话语标记语的元语用分析 [J]．外语教学，2003（4）：16-19.

[63]　吴云．旅游翻译的变译理据 [J]．上海科技翻译，2004（4）：21-24.

[64]　夏翠．从顺应理论看语境在口译中的作用 [J]．理工高教研究，2005（6）：119-120.

[65] 肖龙福．外语教学与文化研究（下）[M]．北京:新华出版社,2005.

[66] 许渊冲．中国古诗精品三百首（汉英对照）[M]．北京:北京大学出版社,2004.

[67] 闫凤霞．中英旅游文本的顺应翻译研究 [D]．济南:山东师范大学（硕士论文）,2007.

[68] 严敏芬．诗歌隐喻共项与诗歌翻译 [J]．外语与外语教学,2002（10）:43-46.

[69] 姚宝荣,梁根顺,魏周．陕西英语导游 [M]．北京:旅游教育出版社,2004.

[70] 杨敏,纪爱梅．英汉旅游篇章的跨文化对比分析 [J]．外语与外语教学,2003（11）:31-35.

[71] 杨青．从语用学角度看结构隐喻在中国电视访谈节目中的顺应性和功能性 [D]．广州:广东外语外贸大学（硕士论文）,2006.

[72] 叶苗．旅游资料的语用翻译 [J]．上海翻译,2005(2):26-28,58.

[73] 曾文雄．语用学综观的文化顺应性翻译美学 [J]．广西社会科学,2006（7）:151-154.

[74] 曾文雄．口译的语用流利性 [J]．中国科技翻译,2002(4):22-24.

[75] 曾文雄．现代电化教育环境下的口译教学 [J]．外语电化教学,2003（4）:46-50.

[76] 周茜．顺应论视角下旅游文本的汉英翻译 [D]．天津:天津商业大学（硕士论文）,2011.

[77] 周昌军,张仲水．齐鲁文化旅游（中英对照）[M]．呼和浩特:远方出版社,2004.

[78] 张德禄．功能文体学 [M]．济南:山东教育出版社,1998.

[79] 张东霞．文本功能转换——论中国旅游手册山水描写的翻译 [D]．广州:广东外语外贸大学（硕士论文）,2006.

[80] 张惠．从跨文化角度谈旅游资料英语翻译 [D]．济南:山东大学（硕士论文）,2005.

[81] 张金荣．通过基于顺应论的阅读教学提高学生的语用意识 [D]．武汉:武汉理工大学（硕士论文）,2006.

[82] 张军益．新闻语言的模糊性及顺应论分析 [D]．上海:上海外国语大学

（硕士论文）,2008.

[83] 张仁霞 . 用社会符号学的理论谈旅游资料的汉译英 [D]. 广州:广东外语外贸大学（硕士论文）,2004.

[84] 张彦敏 . 顺应理论在广告中的应用 [D]. 成都:四川师范大学（硕士论文）,2006.

Appendix 1　Abbreviations

ST: Source Text
TT: Target Text
TT1: Target Text 1
TT2: Target Text 2

Appendix 2   Questionnaire

Age_____   Sex_____   Education_____

Below are six samples of translation on famous scenic spots from home and abroad. Please choose the most suitable version to the source text according to what you've learnt. Then give a brief comment on your choices.

1. 五龙潭

A. Wu Long Tan

B. Wu Long Pool

C. Five-Dragon Pool

D. Five-Tiger Pool

Reasons:

2. 趵突泉

A. Baotu Spring

B. Bao Tu Quan

C. Baotuquan Spring

D. Bubbling Spring

Reasons:

3. 齐烟九点

Context: 齐烟九点引用唐代诗人李贺的诗句"遥望齐州九点烟"来描绘坐落在济南北部的华山、鹊山、凤凰山等九座山头。遥望山头,呈现于晓烟暮霭之中,若隐若现,故态纷呈,故得此名。

A. Nine Pots of Smoke in Qi County

B. The Misty Nine Hills in Qi County

C. Nine Places of Qi County in the Smoke

D. Viewing the Nine Hills of Qi County in the Mist (The number *nine* in

Chinese culture is a popular void denotation to infiniteness.)

Reasons:

4. Starlight on Skyline, Galaxy of Glamour. (an advertisement on Huston)

A. 星星,天河,地平线,如诗如画,令人神往。

B. 点点星光,遥望着地平线;茫茫天河,施展着魔法般的魅力。

C. 星星挂在遥远的天河,向大地散发着无穷的魅力。

D. 高楼摩天,星光灿烂;火树银花,美轮美奂。

Reasons:

5. 紫气东来

A. Ziqi from the East

B. Purple Gas from the East

C. The Noble Wind from the East

D. The Noble Wind from the West

Reasons:

6. 帆船之都

A. The Capital of the Sails

B. The Sails' Capital

C. The Sails' City

D. The Sailing City

Reasons:

Appendix 3　近十年我国旅游文本翻译述评 ^①

　　旅游业是国民经济三大产业之一,可以拉动内需、增加就业、促进国民经济增长,是国家税收的重要来源。随着 2008 年奥运会的举办和上海世博会的召开,中国旅游业迅猛发展,与美国并列成为世界第三大旅游目的地国。作为旅游产品之一,旅游翻译成为近期研究的热点。笔者在中国知网以"旅游翻译"为主题词进行模糊检索,发现近十年来(2001—2010)发表在各期刊上的相关论文有 1 019 篇,硕博士论文 282 篇,会议论文 19 篇。内容涉及面广,角度新颖,但是存在着一些隐性问题,如"重复率高,雷同现象严重,外行参与偏多,学术价值与实际意义不大"(陈刚,2008:1)。文军等在本世纪初曾把旅游翻译中出现的问题归纳为"拼写、遗漏、累赘、中式英语、文化误解"等八类错误(文军,2002:49)。十年过去了,我国的旅游翻译出现了哪些新趋势,又有哪些新问题?笔者将对此梳理,以期为我国的实用翻译理论和教学带来启示。

一、旅游文本翻译的定义

　　国际上对旅游语言的研究起始于英国学者 Graham Dann,他从社会语言学的角度探讨了旅游业语言的特殊性(杨红英,黄文英,2009:104)。国内陈刚教授 2004 年出版了《旅游翻译与涉外导游》,最早对旅游翻译进行了全方位研究,是国内第一本该方面的专著。陈教授认为,旅游翻译是为旅游活动、旅游专业和行业所进行的翻译实践,属于专业翻译,是"一种跨语言、跨社会、跨文化、跨心理的交际活动"(陈刚,2004:259)。语体可分为口头语体和书面语体两种。口头语体主要包括导译,如现编导游词、预制导游词。书面语体指各种旅游文本资料(其中包括口语语体的导译文本)。吕和发重新诠释了旅游翻译的定义、地位和标准,指出,当前全球化语境下的旅游翻译,在整合营销传播理论的指导

---

① 本文原载于《云南农业大学学报(社会科学版)》2013 年第 3 期。收入本书时有所改动。

下,关注的更应是不同功能的动态和静态旅游信息系统及其内部的各个语篇的功能和具体目的间的关联(吕和发,2008:30),由此将旅游翻译分为动态旅游信息(口译)和静态旅游信息(笔译)两大类。限于篇幅,本文所讨论的旅游翻译主要指笔译即旅游文本翻译。旅游文本翻译是指译者为传递景点信息、传播文化知识而进行的旅游书面语篇的专业化翻译活动。国内的旅游文本多指面向外国游客印发的介绍我国旅游资源和风景名胜的文本、光盘,以及对外宣传所用的标识语等。其文体活泼、实用性强、适用范围广。此类旅游文本主要包括旅游指南、旅游宣传手册、解说词、景点介绍、公示语、指示牌、旅游宣传标语、旅游合同、菜单、画册、地图、电子邮件、明信片、光盘。其主要功能是传递信息,诱导游客行动,开展文化传播,满足游客的审美需求。

二、近十年我国旅游文本翻译现状和发展趋势

20 世纪我国的旅游文本翻译,多数从个人主观经验出发,缺乏一定的理论性。进入 21 世纪,一批研究专著的诞生,促进了旅游翻译向专业化发展。陈刚的《旅游翻译与涉外导游》,首次从理论联系实践的角度将“导游”与“翻译”合二为一,阐述了旅游翻译的实践性。金惠康的《跨文化旅游翻译》,对华夏人文传统、传统思想道德、古典文学、诗歌艺术、宗教与民俗文化等特征进行分类介绍,指出旅游翻译要与传播文化结合的特点和规律。在他们的影响下,近十年来(2001—2010)我国旅游翻译方面的论文层出不穷,许多学者从跨学科的角度出发,借鉴国外理论提出了旅游翻译的策略和方法;部分学者结合中国国情提出本土实用翻译模式,主要的发展趋势归结如下。

(一)借鉴国外理论,开展跨学科交叉研究

学者们首先从借鉴国外先进理论入手,用目的指导实践,同时吸收其他学科如语用学、社会语言学及美学等的优秀成果。

1. 德国功能理论

德国功能派理论产生于 20 世纪 70 年代,创始人 Reiss 提出了将文本功能列为翻译批评的一个标准,将文本分为三种类型:信息型、表情型和感染型(张美芳,2006:29)。20 世纪 90 年代初 Nord 进一步完善了该理论,即为了再现原文的预期功能,必要时译者要对译文语篇“进行全面调整,以适应译入语的语篇与文化规范”。德国理论的核心原则是“目的准则”:“任何翻译

行为都是由翻译的目的决定的,简而言之,就是'翻译的目的决定翻译的手段'。"(Nord, 2001:29)

功能理论对旅游文本翻译具有较强的指导意义,它摆脱了传统观念中原文"等值"的束缚,强调了翻译的目的和功能。因此,译者可以根据译文读者的要求,适当地增删甚至改写译文,以符合读者的语言习惯和文化心理。陆国飞选用我国地方旅游景点汉语介绍英译文本,从功能性和实用性两方面对翻译失误加以剖析,论证了译者缺少翻译的目的意识是产生这些失误的根源。张美芳以功能理论尤其是 Reiss 的文本类型学理论为基础,论证了翻译单一功能和复合功能的牌示文本要采用不同的策略。牛新生指出公示语应属于感召型文本,应以译出其感召功能为首要任务,以取得预期的效果。在应用国外理论的文章中,功能理论被应用得最多最广泛,这与旅游文本的自身文本特征及其体现的功能是紧密联系的。

2. 跨文化研究

"旅游翻译是跨文化性质最典型,跨文化特色最鲜明,涉及社会、经济、教育、宗教等因素最多的包罗万象的翻译种类。"(陈刚,2004)尤其是汉语旅游文本中丰富的民间传说、历史掌故、诗词歌赋等,吸引着读者的兴趣,传播了中国文化。杨敏等对比分析了英汉旅游篇章在语势及篇章结构和句式形态、场、元信息等方面的差异,为齐鲁旅游文化的翻译提供了借鉴。汪翠兰从语言特色和风格差异、景点名称和人名的翻译、历史文化词汇的翻译、诗词和古文等文化信息的处理等方面解析了旅游景点翻译的跨文化特征。金惠康总结了跨文化旅游翻译的理据、策略和原则。

3. 语用翻译研究

语用翻译就是通过两种语言形式和内容的对比,在具体的语境中确认话语意义的过程。何自然把语用翻译定义为:"同语义翻译相对应,是一种等效翻译观。它包括语用语言等效翻译和社交语言等效翻译。"(何自然,1995:186)语用翻译强调"语用等效",即在译文读者中产生原文对原文读者类似的感受。李怀奎用实证的方法研究了景观标识名称汉译英的语用等效问题。刘建刚等建议在告示翻译中应该重视语境的作用,增加关联度,扩大认知环境,以达到语用等效目的。

关联理论是语用学中的重要理论,创始人 Sperber 和 Wilson 在著作《关联性:交际与认知》中指出,言语交际是一种有目的、有意识的活动,包含着"明示"和"推理"过程,即听话人用较小的努力获得较大的语境效果(Sperber & Wilson,2001:118)。刘冰泉等利用"最佳关联原则"对涉外导游词《滕王阁》的两个译本进行了分析。叶苗阐释了关联论视角下的旅游资料变异策略,指出四种变异方法即扩充法、缩减法、整编法和替换法有明晰的语用效果。除上述理论外,美学、社会符号学、生态翻译学理论等对旅游翻译都有一定的指导意义。因篇幅所限,不再展开。

(二)从本国国情和实践出发,本土实用翻译理论体系开始建构

国外理论毕竟是"舶来品",不一定适合中国的国情,而我国的"实用翻译理论发展远远落后于实用翻译实践"(林克难,2007:5)。近年来,学者从我国实际出发,积极探索本土翻译理论建设,取得了丰硕的成果。微观策略方面,黄忠廉提出了"变异"理论,即译者根据读者的特殊需求采用扩充、取舍、浓缩、阐释等变通手段摄取原作中心内容或部分内容。林克难提出了"看、易、写"原则,即首先要大量阅读说英语国家的真实材料,仿照其特点变易翻译,最后根据英文同类文本的特点直接用英语撰写文本。而后丁衡祁针对该原则的文化缺陷,补充提出了"模仿、借用、创新"原则,林克难和丁衡祁"打开了实用翻译重视读者反应与译文效果翻译理论建设的新局面,是实用翻译切实可行的一种指导原则"(林克难,2007:8)。同时,学者对译学理论进行了系统整合研究。刘宓庆提出从描写性入手进行整合;杨自俭从逻辑范畴体系入手予以建构,并指出一门成熟的学科理论必须具有自己独有的研究方法论;方梦之则从术语体系角度研究了译学理论整合。在整体理论体系建构的推动下,旅游翻译理论建设走出了一条创新之路。曾利沙提出"旅游指南翻译的主题信息突出策略原则"(曾利沙,2005:19),王东风首创了"语域流变"和"互文干扰"的概念,探讨在语域流变的情况下如何对翻译选择进行风险评估,规避可能出现的消极互文干扰。文军等从语篇功能的角度创建了博物馆解说词适度摘译的基本模式,李德超提出了"旅游英译的平行文本比较模式",以指导酒店文宣的英译。毫无疑问,结合我国翻译实践的本土实用翻译理论更能解决国外理论"水土不服"的弊端,在实践中愈加成熟和完善,是推动译学发展的生力军。

(三)注重传达翻译策略和技巧

策略和技巧的传达一直是实用翻译关注的热点。旅游文本种类多样,特色

鲜明,文化内涵突出,学者们对此提出了不同的翻译策略。刘清波指出了中式菜名英译的技巧和原则,即要正确处理中心词、前置修饰语以及后置修饰语之间的关系,同时要遵循避虚就实、舍繁就简和必要时音译的翻译原则。熊力游探讨了旅游广告汉译英的方法。需要指出的是,公示语翻译成为近年来旅游翻译的热点。北京第二外国语学院公示语翻译研究中心展示了 2005 年夏伦敦实地采集的公示语翻译集锦。戴宗显等以 2012 年奥运会主办城市伦敦为例,指出了在语境全球化条件下公示语汉英翻译应研究遵循的标准。吕和发、丁衡祁等也分别撰文阐释公示语翻译的技巧。

(四)注重调查研究,研究方法逐渐科学,语料库的引入增强了实证性

目前旅游文本的翻译质量参差不齐,究其原因,除了译者的语言学素质千差万别之外,译本多是译者凭着主观经验写成,缺乏实证依据。近年来,学者们注意调查研究,并将社会语言学定性和定量研究的方法引入其中,增强了说服力。文军等用调查问卷调查了不同国家的游客对门票导游图英语介绍中反映的问题的态度。万正方等对上海部分著名路段商店和单位牌名翻译等展开了实地调查。杨红英在研究旅游翻译的可接受度时,向 67 位来华外籍游客作了访谈和实地观察。他们在调查的基础上开展实证研究,避免了主观臆测,同时逐步建立了旅游语篇语料库。李德超介绍了香港理工大学正在研制的新型中英双语旅游语料库及其应用,并进一步论证了基于双语旅游语料库的 DDL 翻译教学。语料库的引入,方便了学者深入开展调查研究,推动了我国旅游翻译的理论和教学工作。然而,成功运用语料库需要一定的社会学统计方法,这就无疑督促广大科研人员与时俱进,努力提高自身科研素质,迎接新技术的挑战。

(五)出现旅游翻译"理论与实践何为第一性"之争鸣

旅游翻译作为实用翻译,究竟是"基于实践"还是"基于理论"的研究,近期学者对此展开了激烈的争论。论战来源于 2008 年《上海翻译》第 3 期的一篇论文:《从翻译理论建构看应用翻译理论范畴化拓展——翻译学理论系统整合性研究之四(以旅游文本翻译为例)》(以下简称《建构》,笔者加)。作者结合旅游指南翻译具体实例,建构了宏—中—微观层次理论范畴体系。陈刚教授对文章进行了批评,认为理论阐述"大费周章","对双语文本的点评和英文改译漏洞较多"(陈刚,2008:5),指出译者因实践量不足导致文质低下,进而提出要

更注重实践研究,文本翻译质量的关键是以实践为基础的对文本信息的专业评价能力和专业翻译能力。而后,《建构》作者从翻译批评的学理性与客观论证性角度展开反驳,认为翻译理论研究与经验法则归纳是可行的,应支持本土理论研究而非盲目沿用西方理论,同时还针对旅游导译中的种种不良现象呼吁遵从商业伦理道德。

理论与实践的关系是翻译研究中的永恒话题。《上海翻译》曾在 2003 年开辟专栏讨论两者关系。许渊冲以《红与黑》首句的翻译为例,指出"实践第一,理论第二",在理论和实践有矛盾的时候,"应该改变的是理论,而不是实践"(许渊冲,2003:2)。而林克难号召"翻译理论需要实践指导",关键是找准切入点,理论与实践可以自然地结合起来。郭建中则认为应"既重视实践,也重视理论",翻译的实践性不应导致对基本理论的轻视或忽视。马克思主义哲学认为,理论的来源是实践,实践是检验认识正确与否的唯一标准;理论对实践有反作用,正确的理论能促进事物的发展。笔者认为,旅游翻译实用性强,必须要有丰富的实践做支撑,实践离不开理论的指导。理论和实践同等重要。正如孙致礼(2003:4)所言,"翻译实践和理论研究都要坚持与时俱进的原则",今后要以实践为基础,以中西方理论为借鉴,推动我国实用翻译建设。

(六)号召旅游翻译规范化

旅游翻译重视信息量的传递,旅游景点的误译势必有损当地形象,阻碍跨文化传播。为此,学者们坚持实事求是的态度,对当前旅游文本翻译中的种种问题予以纠正。吴伟雄指出了我国现行行政区域的英译存在着层级不分与概念混淆的问题,如"地级市"和"县级市"都被翻译成了"city",分不清哪个级别更高;"district"和"office"并为同类,被当作"区域"来介绍;许明武等从词汇、句子和语篇层面分析了中国世界自然文化遗产对外宣传解说中的翻译失误。

旅游翻译的规范化是正确解决当前种种问题的途径。王秋生呼吁"旅游景点翻译亟待规范"(王秋生,2004:79),郭建中指出了某些大城市出台的街道路牌书写的地方法规与国家法律和联合国决议不符的情况,如在过去北京路牌的通名用英语,上海用汉语拼音,重庆则采用了汉英双语标志。他重申了《汉语拼音方案》作为中国地名罗马字母的标准拼写法,号召有关部门依法行事。

值得一提的是,北京第二外国语学院专门成立了公示语翻译研究中心以推动公示语的正规化建设,北京、上海、重庆等地也颁布了公共场所标识语的法规,在他们的带动下,地名翻译等混乱的情况有所改观。旅游翻译的规范化需要各级政府、主管部门的大力支持,才能迎来真正的春天。

三、存在问题

通过上述分析,不难看出近十年来我国的旅游文本翻译取得了一定的进步,从依赖国外理论到本土实用翻译理论体系的构建,从单凭主观经验到定量定性分析的结合,无不渗透着学者的心血,但也暴露出一些问题。

(1)内容角度欠新颖,扎堆现象严重。如在借鉴国外理论的文章中,很多都是从功能理论和跨文化角度展开论述的,层面单一,缺乏新意。某些著名的翻译案例被反复使用,而原创性的、和本地翻译实践结合的译文数量甚少,因此实践性不强,难以推陈出新。

(2)本土实用翻译理论研究略显薄弱,比起应用国外理论的文章少之又少。虽然我国学者在翻译理论方面作出种种探索,并且建构了本国的实用翻译理论体系,但在其影响和引用次数方面大大低于国外理论,国内核心期刊、硕博士论文近年来仍围绕着功能理论等国外理论展开。本土理论只有和我国的旅游翻译实践相结合,向深层次、专业化发展,才能经得起实践的检验。

(3)新兴议题鲜有涉猎。近年来的翻译热点议题如认知翻译等鲜有提及,在目前的认知语言学大潮中略显滞后。

(4)研究方法有待深入。翻译技巧和策略多是主观经验写成;用于调查研究的统计学方法流于表面;而旅游文本翻译的语料库建设我国才刚刚起步。

四、未来旅游文本翻译展望

新世纪的第二个十年刚刚开始,作为对外交流的窗口行业,广大旅游翻译工作者任重而道远。展望未来我国的旅游文本翻译,不难看出以下方面。

(1)跨学科研究进一步加大。研究广泛吸收其他学科如语用学、社会语言学、符号学及认知语言学成果,为旅游翻译提供全新视角。一些旅游翻译的旧话题,如语用翻译,因其灵活性还会有一定的发展空间,而新兴议题的渗透无疑会给旅游翻译带来新的活力。随着认知翻译的热潮在我国的出现,旅游翻译的认知研究增加了。

(2)本土实用翻译理论体系进一步完善,注意和当地旅游景点相结合,一批应用本土理论研究当地旅游景点翻译的论文将会涌现。

（3）翻译的规范化。误译现象逐渐减轻，地名翻译更加统一，遵循相关的国家标准与国际标准，向正规化发展。

（4）语料库语言学兴起对科研工作者的挑战。旅游语篇语料库的逐渐建立，方便了学者展开实证研究。但是广大教师利用语料库和社会统计学方法分析问题的能力还相对欠缺，有的才刚刚接触，这将督促他们努力提高自身科研素质。

参考文献

[1] Nord, Christiane. *Translating as a Purposeful Activity:Functionalist Approaches Explained* [M]. Shanghai:Shanghai Foreign Language Education Press,2001.

[2] Sperber, Dan & Wilson, Deindre. *Relevance:Communication and Cognition*[M]. Beijing:Foreign Language Teaching and Research Press, 2001.

[3] 陈刚. 旅游翻译与涉外导游 [M]. 北京:中国对外翻译出版公司,2004.

[4] 陈刚. 应用翻译研究应是基于实践的研究——以旅游文本及翻译的多样性案例为例 [J]. 上海翻译,2008(4):1-7.

[5] 何自然. 语用学与英语学习 [M]. 上海:上海外语教育出版社,1995.

[6] 黄忠廉. 翻译变体研究 [M]. 北京:中国对外翻译出版公司,2000.

[7] 李德超,王克非. 平行文本比较模式与旅游文本的英译 [J]. 中国翻译, 2009,30(4):54-58,95.

[8] 林克难. 从信达雅、看易写到模仿-借用-创新——必须重视实用翻译理论建设 [J]. 上海翻译,2007(3):5-8.

[9] 吕和发. 旅游翻译:定义、地位与标准 [J]. 上海翻译,2008(1):30-33.

[10] 孙致礼. 理论来自实践,又高于实践 [J]. 上海科技翻译,2003(4):4.

[11] 王秋生. 旅游景点翻译亟待规范 [J]. 中国翻译,2004(3):79-81.

[12] 文军. 信息度与可接受度的统一——对当前旅游翻译的一项调查与分析 [J]. 中国科技翻译,2002(1):49-52.

[13] 许渊冲. 实践第一,理论第二 [J]. 上海科技翻译,2003(1):2.

[14] 杨红英,黄文英. 汉英旅游翻译的可接受性研究 [J]. 外语教学,2009,

30（4）：104-108.

[15] 曾利沙．论旅游指南翻译的主题信息突出策略原则［J］．上海翻译，2005（1）：19-23.

[16] 曾利沙．从翻译理论建构看应用翻译理论范畴化拓展——翻译学理论系统整合性研究之四［J］．上海翻译，2008（3）：1-5.

[17] 张美芳．澳门公共牌示语言及其翻译研究［J］．上海翻译，2006（1）：29-34.

Appendix 4 旅游广告词及语篇语境翻译的语用学阐释：关联－顺应视角 ^①

一、引言

翻译是涉及原文作者、译者和读者三维转换的跨文化交际活动。近年来，翻译研究表现了一些新的发展趋势，如对翻译的定义、地位和分类的重新思考，本土实用翻译理论体系开始建构，多种学科向翻译渗透等，大大拓宽了翻译的研究思路。语用学研究交际中的语言，运用语用学相关理论进行跨学科翻译研究，不拘泥于原文语言形式而对译文进行灵活的变通，实现了与原文的功能对等。

旅游业是"永远朝阳"的第三产业，可以拉动内需、增加就业、促进国民经济增长，也是国家税收的一项重要来源。然而作为旅游产品之一的旅游翻译发展相对滞后，如"重复率高，雷同现象严重，外行参与偏多，学术价值与实际意义不大"（陈刚，2008:1）。因此，本文借助语用学中的关联理论和顺应论，研究旅游篇章的语境翻译问题，以期对旅游翻译理论和实践方面起到指导作用。

二、语用视角下的语境翻译

（一）语用翻译定义

语用翻译就是通过两种语言形式和内容的对比，在具体的语境中确认话语意义的过程。何自然（1997:185）把语用翻译定义为："同语义翻译相对应，是一种等效翻译观。它包括语用语言等效翻译和社交语言等效翻译。语用语言等

---

① 本文原载于《云南农业大学学报（社会科学版）》2012年第1期。收入本书时有改动。

效翻译就是在词汇、语法、意义等语言学的不同层次上不拘泥于原文的形式,只求保存原作的内容,用原文最切近而又最自然的对等语将内容表达出来,以求等效。社交语用等效翻译,则是指为跨语言、跨文化的双语交际服务的等效翻译。"语用翻译强调"语用等效",即在译文读者中产生与原文读者相同的感受。高云和韩丽应用纽马克文本类型和文本功能的划分方法,认为"语用翻译应属交际翻译,而非语义翻译"(高云,韩丽,2004:45)。由于逻辑思维和英汉文化的差异,照直翻译可能会引起种种隔阂,因此,译者可在保持原文关联度的基础上对译文进行灵活的变通,以期达到语用等效。

(二)传统意义的语境观

人类学家 Malinowski 于 1923 年最早提出了"情景语境"的概念,认为"语境对语言理解十分必要",后来又补充了文化语境,丰富和完善了语境的解释(Malinowski,1932)。英国伦敦学派 Firth 继承发展了他的理论,将语境外延扩大,认为不仅包括上下文,还应包括社会环境。20 世纪 70 年代,随着篇章语言学和语用学的发展,美国社会语言学家 Hymes 进一步拓展了语境研究。他认为语境的组成要素包括话语参与者、话题、背景、交际渠道、语码、信息形式、交际事件等。Halliday 对以往的语境理论进行了梳理,认为社会符号系统中的语境特征表现为场、旨和式。总体说来,传统的语境研究认为语境是静态的、已知的,双方按照是否遵从交际原则推理语义,"忽视了交际者在交际过程中选择和创造语境的主动性和语境的动态性"(何兆熊,2000:17),在言语交际过程中可以生成无限话语意义,有些甚至是对原有意义的否定,传统静止的语境观无法对此进行解释。

(三)关联 – 顺应论框架下的语境观

Sperber 和 Wilson 在其重要著作《关联性:交际与认知》中提出了非传统意义的语境观,即认知语境(Sperber & Wilson, 2001:38)。它不限于现实环境中的情景或话语本身的语境,不是交际双方事先知道的,也不是固定不变的,而是动态的。语境是人们在交际互动过程中为了正确理解话语而在大脑中构建的一系列假设,听话人要根据每一个话语内容构建新的语境。由于个体的认知结构不同,话语推理就可以得出不同的隐含结论。关联性是制约人类交际的基本因素,言语交际就是听话人付出最小的努力获得最大效果的明示-推理过程。

但是遗憾的是,作者没有对关联性量化,因而操作性欠佳。比利时国际语用学会会长 Verschueren 适时提出了顺应论,从语用综观的角度阐释语言现象。他认为语言的使用是一个不断的选择语言的过程,不管是有意识的还是无意识的,语言使用者都会作出种种选择,这是因为语言具有商讨性、变异性和顺应性。语言使用过程中的语言选择必须与语境顺应。Verschueren 把语境分为交际语境和语言语境,并提出语境的动态顺应观。顺应论将关联度划分为宏观和微观两个层面,突显了顺应的意识程度,可以更好地解决语言使用和选择过程的语用问题。语用综观的细化使语言分析过程更具操作性,是对关联理论有益的发展和补充。

关联—顺应视角下的语境,是动态生成的,是在人们头脑中生成的种种假设的集合。为了确保言语交际的顺利进行,听话人根据最大关联度的原则不断推翻假设,在逻辑信息、百科信息与词汇信息等方面对话语作出有意识的最佳选择,因此,从根本上讲,话语的生成过程是认知的。

三、关联—顺应论视角下对旅游语篇语境翻译的阐释力

翻译是译者在具备扎实的双语功底的基础上,将源语向目标语转化的跨文化交际活动,其目的就是在译文读者中产生原文对原文读者类似的效果。译者要以"译文读者为中心",在翻译过程中考虑读者的接受度、文化心理、语言习惯和审美能力。

翻译过程可以分为语篇理解和语篇产出两个阶段。(李占喜,2007:3)在语篇理解阶段,译者利用主体认知系统,包括逻辑信息、百科信息与词汇信息等,构建交际双方共知的认知语境假设,推理出与原文话语的最佳关联性,体会原作者的信息和交际意图。其后进行的语篇产出阶段,译者根据互明的认知语境对语言使用作出动态的选择,有意识地顺应读者的交际语境和语言语境。旅游语篇不仅向游客传递着吃穿住行等实用信息,汉语旅游语篇变幻多样的修辞手法、古老优美的历史传说等还满足了游客的审美需求,传播着中国文化。为此,译者必须努力做到以下几点。

(一)顺应物理世界,扩大双方共享的认知语境

译者顺应物理世界主要指对空间和时间指示关系的顺应。空间包括绝对空间关系和参照指示对象的相对空间关系。另外,交际者的体态语、生理特征、

外貌等也属于物理世界的组成部分。地名翻译一直是困扰学者的问题之一,究竟是音译还是意译,学者们对此各抒己见。为此,译界作出了统一要求,翻译地名时,实行"名从主人"的原则,常采用"专名音译,通名意译"的方法。国家法律规定采用汉语拼音将专有地名音译,达到了译名和原名声音上的统一,便于外国游客和当地居民交流,正确寻找旅游地相关信息,宣传我国民族传统文化。另外,翻译中国特有的人文景观时,如亭、台、楼、榭、阁、塔、园、庵等文化意象词,译者还采取直译加注、意译、类比等方法,扩大交际双方的认知语境,减少文化隔阂。时间指示包括事件时间、指称时间和说话时间。请看一例:

例 1 原文:北京故宫耗时 14 年,整个工程于 1420 年结束。(叶苗,2005:26)

译文 1: The construction of the Forbidden City took 14 years, and was finished in 1420, 14 years before Shakespeare was born.

译文 2:…, 72 years before Christopher Columbus discovered the New World.

原文指出了明朝紫禁城(现称故宫)修建的历史意义。众所周知,它是当今世界上现存规模最大、建筑最雄伟、保存最完整的古代宫殿和古建筑群。原文仅有两个数字,外国游客可能无法体会其重要性,译者针对来自不同文化背景的英美游客采取了不同的类比手法,适当增加背景信息。如对英国游客,将故宫完成的时间和英国大文豪 Shakespeare 出生的时间作了一番比较;遇见美国游客时,又灵活地换成了比较熟悉的 Columbus 发现美洲新大陆的事件。这一类比,突出了故宫的建成在中国人心目中的地位,和英国人心中的 Shakespeare、美国人心中的 Columbus 一样举足轻重;同时根据游客的不同文化背景激活了各自的认知语境,扩充了双方的共享知识,游客用最小的努力便能体会到故宫建成的伟大意义,译者的变通更能引起不同文化语境的游客的共鸣。当然,此变通方便了读者,但给译者带来了新的难度与挑战。主要是译者要加强自身的认知语境研习力度。

(二)顺应社交世界,维护交际和谐

高云和韩丽(2004)认为,社交世界指社交场合、社会环境对交际者的言语行为所规范的原则和准则。语言选择受到特定机构的制约,取决于依附关系和权威,或权势和平等关系。中国人讲究"天人合一",促和谐,人与环境和谐共生;西方游客在实用功利主义思想的影响下,崇尚自由,突出个性。因此,译者

要遵循礼貌原则，不"威胁"外国游客的正面和负面面子。

例 2 原文：没去过海底世界，别说到过青岛！

译文 1：Dare not to say you've been to Qingdao without visiting the Underwater World!

译文 2：Welcome to Qingdao Underwater World!

原文是宣传青岛海底世界的一则旅游广告。关联词"没去……别（说）……"可能有两种解释：一是条件性的，如果没去过海底世界，那就别说到过青岛；第二种是因果性的，因为没去过海底世界，所以别说到过青岛。青岛是大海的故乡，不去海底世界看看光怪陆离、千姿百态的海洋生物就愧对青岛之行。

译文 1 采用直译，"Dare not to say..."限制了说话人的权利，"威胁"了西方游客的面子。译文 2 在处理原文歧义时，避开直译，用意译的方法传达邀请功能。"Welcome to..."体现出"好客山东"的特色，有效表达了原文的语用功能。且译文 2 又是在国外对此类广告词最为常见的一种表达方法。

（三）顺应心理世界，满足读者接受度和审美需求

心理世界包括交际双方的个性、情绪、愿望等认知和情感方面的因素。汉语旅游篇章喜用四字成语，讲究字词押韵，排比、拟人、夸张等修辞手法交叉使用，气势磅礴，极具渲染力。英语旅游篇章更注重信息性的表达，用词简明，多向游客提供景点的服务设施、行车路线、交通住宿等。译者应以译文读者为中心，通过增、减、转、述等形式对译文改写，满足不同读者的审美能力和心理期待。

例 3 原文：Here in New Hampshire there are many opportunities to find a peaceful spot hidden among the lush forests of all tall evergreens and hard-woods or next to a rambling brook or pictorial lake.（卢敏，2005）

译文：新罕布什尔州森林茂密，绿树常青，泉水蜿蜒流淌，湖边风景如画，到处都是幽然寂静的好去处。

（四）顺应语言语境，从宏观和微观层面把握对方语言习惯

语言语境体现在篇内衔接、篇际制约和话语的序列安排上。译者不仅要进行语言微观层面的选择，即语音、语调、词汇的选择，还要在宏观层面如语码转

换、文体风格、语篇功能等方面通观全文。英汉旅游篇章在谋篇上各有其特点。在篇章的微观层面,汉语篇章喜用成语,多用修辞,渲染氛围,重视悟性,分句间逻辑关系隐藏在句子内部;英语篇章信息突出、用词简明,重视推理的严密性和逻辑性,小句间关系通过显性的连接词相连。在语篇宏观层面,汉语是螺旋形上升思维,在铺陈渲染之后再引出主要观点;英语是直线型思维,喜欢开门见山,直奔主题而后对其解释。因此,译者要在宏观和微观上把握全文,在语序上对译文结构进行适当的调整。

例 4 原文:在四川的西部,有一处奇妙的去处。它背倚岷山主峰雪宝顶,树木苍翠,花香袭人,鸟声婉转,流水潺潺。它就是松潘县的黄龙。(卢敏,2005)

译文:One peaceful place in the west of Sichuan Province lies at Huang Long in Songpan County. It has lush green forests, filled with fragrant flowers, babbling streams and song birds.

本文借助语用学相关理论,研究了旅游篇章的语境翻译。笔者认为,旅游语篇的翻译语境不是固有的,是动态生成的,是译者根据最大关联度有意识的推理原文假设,继而在向目标语言转化时,在以读者为中心的基础上,顺应读者的物理世界、心理世界、社交世界和语言语境,灵活变通、促进交际和谐的过程。随着时间的推移,这一理论还有待于实践论证。

参考文献

[1] Malinnowski, Bronislaw. *Argonauts of the Western Pacific*[M]. London: G. Routledge and Sons, Ltd. , 1932.

[2] Sperber, Dan & Wilson, Deindre. *Relevance:Communication and Cognition*[M]. Beijing:Foreign Language Teaching and Research Press, 2001.

[3] Verschueren, Jef. *Understanding Pragmatics*[M]. Beijing:Foreign Language Teaching and Research Press, 2000.

[4] 陈刚. 应用翻译研究应是基于实践的研究——以旅游文本及翻译的多样性案例为例 [J]. 上海翻译,2008(4):1-7.

[5] 高云,韩丽. 语用翻译当属交际翻译 [J]. 西安外国语学院学报,2004,12(1):45-47.

[6] 何兆熊. 新编语用学概要 [M]. 上海:上海外语教育出版社,2000.

［7］　何自然.语用学与英语学习［M］.上海:上海外语教育出版社,1997.

［8］　李占喜.关联与顺应:翻译过程研究［M］.北京:科学出版社,2007.

［9］　卢敏.英语笔译实务(2级)［M］.北京:外文出版社,2005.

［10］　叶苗.旅游资料的语用翻译［J］.上海翻译,2005(2):26-28,58.

Appendix 5　旅游城市景点翻译的顺应论诠释 ^①

旅游翻译是近来应用翻译研究的热点话题。随着国民经济的发展,奥运会、世博会的召开,旅游业得到了长足的发展,也给旅游翻译带来了新的契机。

党的十八大以来,国家实施"中国文化走出去"战略,大力弘扬中国文化,提升文化自信和文化软实力。目前,中国文化外译研究主要集中在文学作品的外译上,系统研究中国旅游文化翻译的文章较少,且旅游翻译一直存在着三大问题:过于(脱离实践的)理论化;过于("一刀切"的)规范化;过于经验主义而轻视理论(陈刚,2008:1)。本文以语用学顺应论为理论框架,以奥运会帆船比赛举办城市青岛为例,探讨旅游景点中国文化词语的翻译问题,以期给翻译理论和实践研究带来一定的启示。

一、翻译研究的顺应论视角

(一)顺应论

顺应论认为,无论有没有意识,出于语言内部或外部的原因,语言的使用是持续地选择语言的过程,这是由于语言本身具有变异性、商讨性和顺应性。变异性是"语言提供了多种选择的可能性";商讨性指"说话者并非死板地按形式 - 功能的关系选择语言,而是极其灵活地选择语言策略";顺应性是"人类能从大量的语言变体中,选择出适合交际需要的语言"(Verschueren,2000:56-61)。语言的三个特性是相辅相成、不可分割的。变异性和商讨性是前提和基础,没有它们提供的语言变体,就没有顺应性的发生。顺应性是语言使用的核心,是说话者有意识的动态选择语境的过程。

---

① 本文原载于《青岛职业技术学院学报》2017 年第 6 期。收入本书时有所改动。

（二）语境的动态顺应

古希腊的 Aristotle 曾指出词语的意义依赖于语境，但首次明确提出"语境"概念的却是波兰人类学家 Malinowski，他认为语境应包括"文化语境"和"情景语境"。伦敦学派 Firth 在此基础上将语境分为语言和情景的上下文。系统功能语言学家 Halliday 认为 Firth 的定义有些狭窄，还应包括语音语调等文化方式，他提出了"语域"的概念，将其分为语场、语旨和语式。认知语言学家 Sperber 和 Wilson 认为"语境是听话人对世界的认知假设"。为获得最佳关联性，说话人力图让听话人以最小的努力取得最大的语境效果。但是关联理论的"语境"观没有具体指出语境在哪些层面发挥作用，因此操作性欠佳。在此基础上，Verschueren 提出了顺应论的语境观。他把语境分为交际语境和语言语境。前者分为物理世界、心理世界和社交世界，后者指根据语境选择的各种语言手段。Verschueren 认为语境是动态的，是说话人有意识的选择语言的过程。

（三）顺应论和翻译

翻译是涵盖原作者、译者和译文读者的三维转换活动。译者发挥主体性，不仅要顺应原文语境，获取最大关联性，还要顺应目标语读者的语言语境、文化语境和社会规范，满足出版社、赞助商和读者的诗学和意识形态需求。顺应论无疑为翻译研究提供了理论框架和可操作模式，它将语境细化为物理、心理、社交和语言语境，翻译的过程变成译者发挥主体间性、顺应源语和目标语语境和语言结构的过程。

国内顺应论视角下的翻译研究也取得了一系列进展。理论研究层面，宋志平认为顺应论提供了翻译研究的框架，拓宽了翻译研究的发展空间。王建国指出翻译方法（如直译、意译、归化、异化）都是译者主动地或者被动地顺应原文的方法。实践层面，孟健等通过研究辜鸿铭英译《论语》，指出译者需顺应文化差异，弥补文化缺省，才能弥补信息传递障碍。张绍全等研究了顺应论视阈中法律文本翻译过程的呈现效度。综上所述，顺应翻译研究的理论探讨较多，结合当地旅游景点翻译的文章较少，因此，笔者以帆船之都青岛为例，探讨顺应论视角下旅游景点翻译的方法和策略，以传播城市文化，构建良好的城市形象。

二、"中国文化走出去"战略背景下城市景点翻译的顺应论诠释

旅游翻译是为旅游业、旅游活动、大专院校等提供专业服务的实践活动。

它属于应用翻译,可以分为书面语体的旅游文本翻译和口语语体的导游翻译。旅游文本种类众多,包括旅游景点介绍、旅游指南、公示语、旅游明信片、旅游城市宣传片、外宣材料、菜谱等。鉴于篇幅,本文的研究对象为基于书面语体的城市旅游景点的翻译,选用的语料来自实地拍照、旅游专著、正规出版物和旅游局官网等。

按照语言的功能,语篇体裁分为表情类、信息类和呼唤类文本(Newmark,2001:40)。中英旅游文本在文体特征、语言结构和功能等方面存在差异,译者应充分发挥其主体性,适当采取增添、删减、直译加注等方法,顺应读者的阅读期待和需求。旅游语篇中译者的顺应表现为物理世界、心理世界、社交世界和语言语境的顺应。

(一)物理世界的顺应

物理世界多指时间和空间指示词,也包括交际双方的手势、眼神和外貌等因素(Verschueren,2000:95)。体态语主要运用在口头交际的现场导游翻译中,书面语体出现的频率很少,不属于本文的研究范围。旅游文本中译者对物理世界的顺应主要体现在时间指示词和地名的处理上。

1. 时间指示词

Verschueren 把时间指示词分为表示相对关系的说话时间、指称时间和绝对的事件时间。翻译时应理清指示关系,必要时添加信息增加语境关联。

例1 原文:如果你曾去过慕尼黑啤酒节,那么也该光临每年 6 月份在青岛举行的亚洲啤酒节,品尝品尝那里的啤酒味道如何;……这里最早的啤酒厂,建于 1897—1915 年间,许多啤酒专家把青岛啤酒誉为亚洲之冠。(马会娟,2014:123)

译文:If you've already been to Munich's famous Oktoberfest, it's time to try the Asian version—the Summer Beer Festival in Qingdao each June—The original breweries were built between 1897 and 1915 when Qingdao was a German treaty port and many connoisseurs feel that the city produces the best beer in Asia.

一年一度的"青岛啤酒节"被称为"亚洲最大的啤酒盛会",虽已举办了 20 多年,很多国外游客对此并不熟悉,因此译者首先将青岛啤酒节和慕尼黑啤酒节进行了一番类比,称其为德国慕尼黑啤酒节的"亚洲版本"(Asian version),拉近了和外国游客的距离。当涉及游客不甚熟悉的时间指示词 1897—1915 年时,译者增添了部分文化背景常识,特指 1898 年《胶澳租借条约》签订后,青岛处于德国租借管理时期,突出了青岛啤酒在酿造工艺和口感方面的德国风味。同时,译者选用了中性词"treaty"(合约)描述了青岛被德国统治的时期,称之为"合约期",淡化了它被西方管辖的殖民色彩,容易被西方游客所接受。

2. 地名的处理

地点指示词的翻译在旅游语篇中主要表现为地名的翻译。地名翻译是应用翻译中的一大难点,译名不统一容易引起游客理解的困难。国家近年来陆续出台了地名翻译的国家标准,即应遵从"名从主人"原则,专名音译,通名意译。但遇到特定文化内涵的地名时,应灵活采用多种方法。

例 2　原文:五四广场

译文 1:Wusi Square

译文 2:May 4th Movement Square(to commemorate the sovereignty movement against imperialism and feudalism in 1919)

五四广场是青岛的标志性建筑,因五四运动而得名,广场中央有红色火焰标志"五月的风",象征着青岛是五四运动的导火索。译文 1 采取的音译法虽然简单易记,却难以突出其文化内涵;译文 2 先用意译法指出"五四广场"的渊源,而后解释了五四运动的反帝反封建特征,也向外国友人宣告了青岛主权的神圣和不容侵犯。

例 3　原文:八大关

译文 1:Eight Great Gates/Entrances

译文 2:Badaguan

译文 3:Badaguan Scenic Areas(the eight roads named after the great passes of the Great Wall)

查阅《新华字典》,我们发现"关"是指古代因犯戴枷锁时脖子或手脚穿过刑具,意指拘禁,引申为设在险要地方和边境上防止入侵的关口,即关隘,常指险要的关口。如《南齐书·萧景先传》:"惠朗依山筑城,断塞关隘。"毛主席曾作"雄关漫道真如铁,而今迈向从头越"。青岛的"八大关"有八条马路(实为十条),以中国古代八大著名的关隘命名,如山海关、嘉峪关、居庸关。如今八大关因有康有为、梁实秋、老舍等名人故居、欧式建筑等发展为著名的旅游景区,体现了青岛"红瓦绿树、碧海蓝天"的城市特色(康有为语)。译文 1 把"关"译成"gate"或"entrance"都不太合适,没有突出"关"之险和防御功能,不如译为"pass"(a means as an opening, a road, or a channel by which a barrier may be passed or access to a place may be gained)。译文 2 采用了音译的方法,游客无法领会其深刻的文化内涵。译文 3 采用了"音译 + 注释"的方法,先音译,并用意译法指出其实际为旅游景区"Scenic Areas",而后解释说明了八大关的名字来源于古代长城的八大关隘,加深了景点的文化底蕴。

译者从语言功能出发,对含有文化内涵的地名采取意译的方法,还体现在以下地名的翻译中,如栈桥(the Zhanqiao Pier),小青岛(Xiaoqingdao Park),"崂山十二景"中的海峤仙墩(the Rock of Eight Immortals)、龙潭喷雨(Longtan Waterfall)、太清水月(the Moon Reflected by the Bay near Taiqinggong Palace)、华楼叠石(the Piled-up Stones in Hualou Peak)。

(二)心理世界的顺应

心理世界指情感、愿望、感知和认知等心理因素。美国心理学家马斯洛于 1943 年提出了需求层次理论,将人类需求分为生理、社交、安全、尊重和自我实现需求。来华旅游的国外游客多数是中产阶级,阅读旅游文本的目的是获取旅游信息,愉悦身心,获得审美体验。译者应"贴近国外受众的思维习惯"(黄友义,2004:27)。中外游客的差异主要表现为审美心理,文化心理和意识形态层面上。

1. 审美心理

中国传统哲学讲究"天人合一"。人应顺应天命,达到和大自然的和谐统一。汉语旅游文本以呼唤型文本和表情型文本为主,借山水或抒情或言志,情景交融,物我两忘,"一切景语皆情语",语言形式讲究工整对仗,成语、古诗词、排比等增添了语言的形、音、意之美;而西方哲学主张人与自然的对立,主观和客观分离,轻主观感受,重逻辑思辨。英语旅游文本以信息型文本和呼唤型文本为主,语言平实不夸张,国外游客更多关注的是景点名称、旅游路线、食宿等实用信息,为此译者需灵活变通以满足国外游客的审美需求。

例 4 原文:(崂山)以巨峰为中心,层峦叠嶂之间,奇石林立、幽洞密布、流泉清吟、花木扶疏,更有大量古老的宫观寺庙,为这座道教名山增加了几分宗教的神韵。(周雯,2009:54)

译文：Among range upon range of peaks in Laoshan, there are marvelous stones, caves, streams, springs, plants as well as numerous old Taoist temples.

原文画线部分四个成语组成排比结构，"奇石""幽洞""流泉""花木"对偶句描绘出了山清水秀的自然风光，"立、布、吟、疏"隔行押韵，极富音美、形美和意美，但对于追求旅游信息性的外国游客看来，过分渲染的评价性词汇反而显得华而不实，因此译者只摘译了其中的景观，去掉了过多的修饰语，注重了信息度的表达。

2. 文化心理

旅游翻译是跨文化交际活动，中外游客在思维方式、价值观念和意识形态等方面存在着差异，译者需顺应游客的文化认知语境，减少交际障碍。汉语旅游语篇中诗词、典故等增添了知识性、艺术性，妥善处理好上述文化特色词语，将有利于传播中国文化。在中国文化走出去的背景下，旅游外宣翻译应以中国文化传播为主体，以国外游客的需求为导向，采取增添、转换、删减等方法，顺应游客的心理期待。

第一，诗词。

例 5　原文："烟水苍茫月色迷，渔舟晚泊栈桥西；乘凉每至黄昏后，人依栏杆水拍堤。"这是诗人赞美青岛海滨的诗句。青岛是一座风光秀丽的海滨城市，夏无酷暑，冬无严寒。（康宁，2005：38）

原译：Qingdao is a charming coastal city, whose beauty often appears in poetry. It is not hot in summer or cold in winter.

改译：As an ancient poem put it, "In a haze, lost in the moonlight, moored the fishing boat dimly at night; At dusk , in the breeze in the west of Zhanqiao Pier, lean on the handrail with tide ebb and flow." Qingdao is a charming coastal city which is neither hot in summer nor cold in winter.（笔者译）

汉语诗句中"迷""西""后""堤"组成押韵结构，描绘出黄昏时分栈桥烟波浩渺、清爽宜人的静谧之美。"泊""依""拍"三个动词使得动静结合，相得益彰。原译文直接把诗文删除，概括译为"青岛是个美丽的海滨城市"，原文的意境之美大打折扣，难以引起读者的共鸣，且"旅游翻译如果一味把对联、古诗词等文化负载词删减不译，将不利于中国文化的宣传"（邹建玲，2013：48）。因此，笔者尝试将汉语诗译出，兼顾了英文诗歌的押韵，栈桥之美跃然纸上。

第二,文化典故。

例 6　原文:……但李诗宛如姑射仙子,有一种落花流水之趣,令人可爱。(沈复,2009:20)

译文:but Li Po's Poems have the wayward charm of a Nymph. His lines come naturally like dropping petals and flowing waters, and are so much lovelier for their spontaneity.(林语堂译)

原文摘自《浮生六记》,是清朝长洲人沈复的自传体小说,记述了夫妻俩游览各地的见闻。"姑射"是山名,《庄子·逍遥游》记载:"藐姑射之山,有神人居焉;肌肤若冰雪,淖约若处子。"后多喻指神仙或美人。芸娘认为李白的诗像姑射仙子,不事雕琢,浑然天成,体现了自然可爱的神韵。林语堂先生赞其为"中国文学中最可爱的女人",翻译时他巧妙借用了古希腊神话 Nymph 的形象。Nymph 是居于山林水泽中的美丽仙女,能歌善舞,崇尚自由,和姑射仙子形象接近,比直译"a beauty"更能衬托出姑射仙子的品性。

旅游语篇中文化典故的借用,减少了读者处理文化常识所需的努力,激活了读者的文化认知语境,更能引起读者的认同感。类似的例子还有把西施比作"Cleopatra"(埃及艳后),把《水浒传》中的绿林好汉比作"Chinese Robin Hood",把青岛比作"东方的瑞士"(Eastern Switzerland)等。

第三,政治意识形态。法国哲学家 Destutt de Tracy 在 1796 年首次提出了"意识形态"(Roucek,1944:479)。马克思主义认为,意识形态反映了当权者或者主流的价值观念。遇到意识形态等敏感词汇时,译者需要进行适度改写。著名翻译理论家 Susan Bassnet 与 Lefevere(1990:9)指明:"翻译当然是对原作的改写……改写是一种操纵,是为权力服务的。"方梦之(2011)指出,翻译是双重权力话语制约下的再创造活动;不同政治语境下,同样的现象会有不同的说法。因此,译者需要保持高度的政治敏锐性,在坚持国家主权的基础上,对含有某些意识形态的词语进行适当改写。

(三)社交世界的顺应

社交世界指交际双方主动遵守的准则和社会行为规范。在中国城市旅游景点翻译中,可以看到类似"禁止随地吐痰""禁止大声喧哗""禁止插队"等中英文公示语翻译,而在某些国家,公共场合不吐痰、不插队、不大声喧哗等已经成为约定俗成的规则,刻意突出反而使游客不习惯,因此此类标语可以删减不译。

例 7　原文:没到过海底世界,别说到过青岛!

译文:Welcome to Qingdao Underwater World!

本例是来自青岛海底世界的广告词,从字面意义来看,作者想说去过青岛的人都到过海底世界,利用游客的从众心理劝说游客游玩,但从语气上说,汉语采用的是祈使语气,连接词"没……别说……"表达了命令和劝说功能,言外之意为"连海底世界都没去过,还算了去了青岛呢?",隐含了对外地游客的轻视。如果将原文直译为祈使句,译文生硬、不友好,因此译者从语用功能出发,改译为国外常用的表达欢迎功能的语句,促进了人际交往的和谐。

(四)语言语境的顺应

语言语境,指语言运用的上下文,包含语篇衔接、篇际制约和线性序列。由于英汉旅游语篇逻辑连接方式和组篇方式的不同,译者需顺应国外读者语言语境进行改写,使译文更具连贯性。

例 8　原文:青岛地理位置得天独厚,一面为陆,东北部群山环绕,如屏障拱卫;三面环海,面对黄海与胶州湾,有众多的岬角、海湾,而且一年四季不冻不淤,是一座著名的良港和驰名中外的避暑胜地。

译文:Qingdao is a well-known good harbour and summer resort for its unique geographical location. On its northeast side is the land surrounded by mountains like a protective screen; the other three sides embrace the sea with numerous capes and bays facing the Yellow Sea and Jiaozhou Bay. Furthermore, it is neither frozen nor silted up all the year round.

(笔者译)

汉语思维多迂回性,在语篇层面习惯先铺垫,结论性的内容放在最后;英语思维呈直线形,将结论性的句子放在前面作为主题句,再展开说明原因。例句中汉语原文的主题句放在最后一句,译文按照英美人士的习惯调整语序放在句首将其作为主题句。汉语分句主位结构松散,主位不一致,显得比较零乱;译者调整后使之具有同一主位 Qingdao,衔接自然连贯;利用连接词"On its northern east side…, on the other three sides, Furthermore"表明了分句间的并列和递进关系。将三个短句"三面……面对……有……"处理为带有分词 ing 结构和 with 介词短语的长句,层次分明,重点突出。

四、结论

顺应论是语用综观论,从语言维度、交际维度和心理维度研究语言现象,为旅游翻译研究提供连贯统一的框架。顺应论视角下的旅游翻译,将翻译中的语言和文化研究结合起来,克服了"文化转向"的片面性。在"中国文化走出去"的背景下,旅游翻译应努力做到以下两点。

(1)以中国文化传播为主导,提升文化自信。对文化负载词语(culturally-loaded words),译者可以通过直译加注、脚注或尾注、音译加注释、删减等方法,让读者多层次了解中国文化。

(2)旅游翻译不应忽视读者的信息、文化心理和社交需求,应尽量减少文化隔阂,满足读者的阅读期待。

语用顺应论为旅游翻译提供了一种视角,能否被大多数的游客接受,仍需经过实践检验。物理世界顺应中的人称指示词如 you 在英汉旅游语篇中的处理,地名翻译的多样性和复杂性,文化负载词的翻译方法能否为国外友人所接受等,都是今后深入发展的议题。本文的观点能否得到旅游语篇数据库和实验统计方法的验证,有待进一步考察。

参考文献

[1] Susan, Bassnett & Lefevere, Andrew. *Translation*, *History and Culture*[M]. London and New York:Pinter, 1990:9.

[2] Newmark, Peter. *Approaches to Translation*[M]. Shanghai:Shanghai Foreign Language Education Press, 2001.

[3] Roucek, Joseph. A history of the Concept of Ideology[J]. *Journal of the History of Ideas*, 1944(4):479-488.

[4] Verschueren, Jef. *Understanding Pragmatics*[M]. Beijing:Foreign Language Teaching and Research Press, 2000.

[5] 陈刚. 应用翻译研究应是基于实践的研究——以旅游文本及翻译的多样性案例为例[J]. 上海翻译, 2008(4):1-7.

[6] 方梦之. 论翻译生态环境[J]. 上海翻译, 2011(1):1-5.

[7] 国家历史文化名城研究中心. 中国历史文化名城——青岛[M]. 北京:中国铁道出版社, 2009.

[8]　黄友义.坚持"外宣三贴近"原则,处理好外宣翻译中的难点问题[J].中国翻译,2004(6):27-28.

[9]　康宁.从语篇功能看汉语旅游语篇的翻译[J].中国翻译,2005(3):88.

[10]　马会娟.汉英文化比较与翻译[M].北京:中国对外翻译出版有限公司,2014.

[11]　沈复.浮生六记[M].林语堂,译.北京:外语教学与研究出版社,2009.

[12]　周雯.美丽的青岛[M].北京:中国旅游出版社,2009.

[13]　邹建玲.旅游翻译研究1998—2012年综述——基于人文类核心期刊语料分析[J].中国科技翻译,2013(4):48-51.

[14]　邹卫宁,译.青岛•中国最具魅力的海滨城市[M].青岛:青岛出版社,2009.

Appendix 6　翻译的顺应性研究 ①

一、引言

　　翻译是从源语言向目标语转换的复杂性活动,涉及原作者、译者和读者三维因素,因此译者扎实的双语语言知识、丰富的文化意识和广博的百科知识起着十分重要的作用。长期以来,由于缺乏统一的翻译理论标准,译界在如何评价译文质量的问题上争鸣不断。近几年重新兴起的"归化""异化"之争,以及女性主义在翻译中主体地位的体现等等,都从不同的侧面反映了翻译的特征。但是,统一理论的缺失必会导致译本的千变万化,给译文质量的评价带来了难度。比利时的国际语用学会秘书长 Verschueren 于 1999 年提出了顺应论(Adaptation Theory),从语用综观的角度研究语言现象。这一理论有很强的解释力,可以解释话语标记语、语码转换等现象。因此,笔者也借助这一顺应论研究翻译,提出顺应论指导下的翻译模式,希望能给翻译研究增加一定的理论意义和实践意义。

二、语言学和翻译研究综述

　　目前翻译理论的研究主要从七个方面进行:语言学视角、文艺学视角、文化学视角、交际学视角、行动目的论视角、多元系统视角和解构主义视角(胡庚申,2004:21-23)。七种视角各有千秋,又有各自的局限性。单从语言学视角来看,较早从语言学角度研究翻译的是布拉格学派语言学家 Roman Jakobson。1959年,他在《论翻译的语言问题》中区分了三种翻译:语内翻译、语际翻译和符际翻译。美国的 Eugene Nida 博士在 1964 年和 1969 年先后出版了《翻译科学探索》和《翻译理论与实践》两部翻译著作,提出了"动态对等"的概念,以后发展为

---

① 本文原载于《文教资料》2007 年 2 月。收入本书时有改动。

"功能对等",并把读者对译文的反应看成是检验译文质量高低的标准。他的理论不仅仅在语义层面上,而且更注重翻译中的语用和交际因素。随后,美国的Newmark在此基础上提出了交际翻译和语义翻译的理论,认为"交际翻译试图对译文读者产生与原文对原文读者所产生的效果尽可能接近的效果。语义翻译试图在译语的语义与句法结构允许的范围内,尽可能贴切地传达原文的准确的语境意义"。20世纪80年代,随着语用学作为一门独立的学科的兴起,其强大的实用性对翻译研究产生了较大的影响。语用学的各个领域,比如指示语、预设、礼貌、会话含义、关联理论、言语行为理论和话语分析,都可以为翻译研究提供科学的、微观的语用学分析方法。Leo Hickey于2001年出版了《语用学与翻译》一书,里面收录了13篇论文,分别从语用学的上述角度阐释了语用因素对翻译者和翻译实践的制约和影响。近年来,关联理论成为语用学研究的一大热点,较系统研究关联理论和翻译关系的是Wilson的学生Gutt,他在博士论文《翻译与关联:认知与语境》中提出了关联翻译的理论,将翻译看成是对源语进行阐释的明示-推理活动,译者通过译文将自己的认知图示与译文读者进行交流。顺应论产生后,引起了我国学者的广泛关注。陈喜华(2001)提出语境顺应的观点,认为翻译时必须统观全文,把握好语境的顺应。戈玲玲(2002)利用顺应论的框架,说明翻译是一个在源语的语境和语言结构之间作出顺应的动态过程。宋志平(2004)指出翻译是动态的选择过程,是"译者在元语用意识支配下对语作出调整和商议的自我调控过程"。由此可见,顺应论对翻译具有强大的解释力。在此,笔者也想借助于顺应论研究翻译问题,希望在理论和实践上给翻译研究带来新的启示。

三、顺应论和翻译

(一)顺应论

1.顺应论的理论基础

Darwin在1859年《物种起源》一书中,认为生物进化大体包含生物变异、生存适应、物种进化三个基本的概念。生存适应是指生命体对于环境、生活条件的适应是普遍存在的,因此生命体适应自然环境的基本规律是汰弱留强,适者生存。Verschueren在《语用学新解》中接受了Darwin的观点,认为语言同样有适应性的特征,表现为语言具有选择性、适应性和顺应性等特征。

2. 顺应论概述

比利时国际语用学会秘书长 Verschueren 在他的新著《语用学新解》（2000）中提出了语用学是语言的一种综观的观点。在此基础上,他还提出了"顺应论",以全新的观点去理解诠释语用学。他认为,语言的使用是一个不断选择语言的过程,不管是有意识的还是无意识的,语言使用者都会作出种种选择,这是因为语言具有商讨性、变异性和顺应性。语言的变异性是指语言具有一系列可供选择的可能性;商讨性指所有的选择都不是机械地严格按照形式一功能的关系作出的,而是在高度灵活的原则和策略基础上完成的;顺应性是指语言能够让其使用者从可供选择的项目中作灵活的变通,从而达到成功的交际。根据语用学综观论和顺应论,语言使用要在四个方面顺应:语境关系、语言结构、顺应的动态性和顺应过程的意识程度。

（二）顺应论对翻译的启示

翻译是一种特殊的语言现象,涉及源语言和目标语言的语码转换过程,因而好的译文必须能够在语言结构、语体风格、文化意识等方面契合原文,达到功能方面的动态对等。顺应论中的语用综观论无疑为翻译研究提供了框架,为系统的研究翻译指明了方向。因此,笔者借助于顺应论框架,从语言结构、语境关系、动态的意识顺应等方面研究译文是如何顺应原文的风格和结构的。

四、顺应论在翻译中的应用

（一）语境的顺应

Verschueren 把语境分为交际语境和语言语境。交际语境由物理世界、心理世界和社交世界组成。语言语境也称为信息通道,指语言在使用过程中根据语境选择的各种语言手段。下面,笔者结合翻译实例,阐释语境顺应是如何影响翻译的,所用的语料来自翻译研究丛书及翻译理论研究专著。

1. 物理世界的顺应

物理世界中最重要的因素是时间和空间的指示关系。时间指示包括事件时间、指称时间和说话时间。空间包括绝对空间关系和参照指示对象的相对空间关系。另外,交际者的体态语、生理特征、外貌等也属于物理世界的组成部分。译者在翻译时,要充分考虑到原文作者和读者之间在物理世界中的差异,以便让读者更清楚地理解原文。比如在表达"四面"的顺序时,中国人习惯于先说"东西",后说"南北";在谈到纵向的两个方位时,中国人习惯于先说"南",再说"北",如"南征北战""一桥飞架南北,天堑变通途"。英美人习惯于先说"北",后说"南",如"fly north and south(转战南北)"。在表示八方的方位时,汉语中的"东北"在英语中成了"northeast"。

例 1　原文:But we are getting ahead of the story.

译文:可是我们已经说到故事的后面去了。(包惠南,2001:32)

英语中 ahead 指将要发生的时间,如 go ahead(继续往下说!),而在汉语中的时间副词中,"前"指过去,"后"指未来的时间。唐代文学家陈子昂在《登幽州台歌》中写道:"前不见古人,后不见来者,念天地之悠悠,独怆然而涕下。"所以,在翻译实践中,译者要注意英汉双语在物理世界指示词上的差别,更好地顺应原文。

2. 社交世界的顺应

社交世界指社交场合、社会环境对交际者的言语行为所规范的原则和准则。由于中英两国历史文化传统、社会心理、风俗习惯等的不同,两者在社会规范和社交礼仪等方面存在者巨大的差异。因此,译者要有高度的文化敏感度,深刻洞察社交差异,以便准确真实地再现原文。例如,在请别人吃饭时,主人费力做了一桌丰盛的饭菜,在招呼客人时说下面的话。

例 2　原文:今天饭菜不好,请多包涵。来,先干上一杯。(包惠南,包昂,2004:23)

译文:There are best dishes we're able to prepare. Please make yourself at home. Now, to everyone, cheers!

这是主人在招呼客人时常用的客套话。说"饭菜不好"并不是说饭菜的质量差劲,而是中国人谦虚、不自夸品质的体现。英美人则相反,他们把自己的成就、别人对自己的赞扬看成是对自己能力的肯定,因此他们乐意向朋友展示自己的技艺。所以在翻译时,要顺应两国不同的社交礼仪,译文中使用了"best dishes"一词。

3. 心理世界的顺应

心理世界包括交际双方的个性、情绪、愿望等认知和情感方面的因素。顺应读者的心理世界,有利于读者更好地理解原文的内涵。

例 3　原文:(赵辛楣)一肚皮的酒,几乎全化成酸醋……（钱锺书,1991）

译文: The wine in Xinmei's stomach turned to sour vinegar in his jealousy.

在中国,"醋"不仅是一种调味品,还有丰富的语义内涵,"吃醋"表示看到喜欢的人和别人在一起心生妒忌,而在英美文化中"醋"仅是调味品,所以译者在译文中加上了"in his jealousy",这样外国读者才能体会到赵辛楣心理的变化。

4. 语言语境的顺应

语言语境即我们通常所说的上下文,它包括篇内衔接、篇际制约和线性序列。翻译时注意把握原文的文体风格,并注意上下文之间的衔接和连贯。

例 4　原文: The existence of giant clouds was virtually required for the Big Bang, first put forward in the 1920's, to maintain its reign as the dominant explanation of the cosmos.

译文:宇宙大爆炸理论是 20 世纪 20 年代首次提出的,在解释宇宙起源的诸多理论中,这一理论占主导地位。而巨星云的存在学说对于该理论又几乎是不可缺少的。(卢敏,2005)

英文原文习惯将最重要的内容放在句首,其他小句对其进行解释说明。翻译时译者按照宇宙大爆炸理论出现的时间先后顺序将句子重新排列,最后指出了其重要性,译文显得自然、通畅,更符合中国人的思维习惯。

（二）语言结构的顺应

语言结构的顺应指从多方面对话语作出选择:选择语言、语码、语体,选择话语的构建成分,选择不同类型的话语和语段,选择话语的构建原则。因此,翻译不仅要进行语言微观层面的选择,即语音、语调、词汇的选择,还要在语码转换、文体风格等宏观层面通观全文。如科技语体的翻译尽量采用直译,采用正式化的书面语言,以准确表达条款内容为主要原则;广告、旅游语体抒情词语较多,翻译时应在准确的基础上力求措辞优美,展现原文的风格;文学作品的翻译要突出其文学观赏性。

（三）翻译是有意识的动态顺应

翻译是有意识、有目的的活动,译者要顺应原文的时间、语境、语言结构,结合文化背景、双语知识对译文作出相应的调整。交际者在选择语言时表现出来的自我意识反映,是元语用意识。翻译就是不断对话语作出调整和商议的过程。例如在口译中,译员根据发言人讲话的风格调整自己的语言,在语速、词汇等方面顺应讲话人的语言结构。

例5　原文:中国也准备作出最大的让步。(莫爱屏,2005)

译文:China is prepared to make the biggest concession within its ability.

"最大的让步"语气过强,照直翻译可能会给国家带来损失,译者在处理时灵活地加上了"within its ability",避免了绝对意义,又挽回了说话人的面子。可见,译员在翻译过程中保持清醒的头脑、动态地顺应原文是何等的重要。

(四)翻译要顺应读者的反馈

翻译的最终目的是让读者更好地了解源语文化。Eugene Nida 博士曾把读者的反馈看成是评价译文质量高低的标准。译文究竟能不能经得起时间的考验,还得由读者的反应来证明。一篇译文,尽管文笔优雅,洋洋洒洒数千字,读者读后却不知所云,不能称得上是好译文。因此,译者要充分考虑到读者的文化背景、认知心理、语言知识等因素,提倡百家争鸣,让目标语读者阅读不同的译文,把读者的反应作为评价译文好坏的重要因素,以此来推动译界的发展。从另一方面来讲,不同译者之间的竞争,本身就是顺应论的体现。

五、翻译模式框架及结论

综上所述,借助于语用学的顺应论,我们可以解决翻译学的理论和实践问题。笔者试着将顺应翻译的模式总结如下:

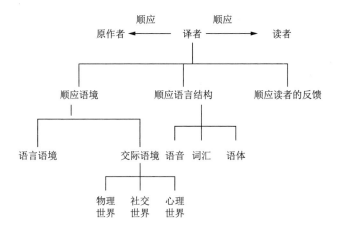

上述模式对翻译研究有着较强的理论和实践意义。翻译是涉及原作者、译者、读者的三维活动。在进行翻译时，译员要顺应原文的语境、语言结构和读者的反馈。顺应语境是指顺应原文的语言语境、物理世界、心理世界和社交世界；顺应语言结构就要从语音、词汇、语体等方面入手；同时在产出语言时，又要顺应目标语读者的心理期待，注重读者的反馈。因此，顺应是双向的，贯穿于翻译过程的始终。应用这一模式，我们可以解决不同文体的翻译问题。在宏观方面，要顺应原文的语体风格、语境和读者的反馈；微观方面，要从语音、语调、词汇等方面开始。只有将宏观、微观结合起来，才能更有效地顺应原文，实现真实、对等的翻译。

参考文献

[1]　Hickey, Leo. *The Pragmatics of Translation* [M]. Shanghai: Shanghai Foreign Language Education Press, 2001.

[2]　Verschueren, Jef. *Understanding Pragmatics* [M]. Beijing: Foreign Language Teaching and Research Press, 2000.

[3]　陈喜华. 试论翻译中的语境顺应 [J]. 湖南大学学报(社会科学版), 2001 (4): 158-160.

[4]　包惠南. 文化语境与语言翻译 [M]. 北京: 中国对外翻译出版公司, 2001.

[5]　包惠南, 包昂. 中国文化与汉英翻译 [M]. 北京: 外文出版社, 2004.

[6]　戈玲玲. 顺应论对翻译研究的启示——兼论语用翻译标准 [J]. 外语学刊, 2002(3): 7-11.

[7]　胡庚申. 翻译适应选择论 [M]. 武汉: 湖北教育出版社, 2004.

[8]　卢敏. 英语笔译实务(2级) [M]. 北京: 外文出版社, 2005.

[9]　莫爱屏. 国际交流中口译语体的语用分析与顺应选择 [J]. 江西科技师范学院学报, 2005(2): 79-83.

[10]　钱锺书. 围城 [M]. 北京: 人民文学出版社, 1991.

[11]　宋志平. 翻译: 选择与顺应－语用顺应视角下的翻译研究 [J]. 中国翻译, 2004(2): 19-23.